JOHN FOWLER

THE INVENTION OF THE
COUNTRY-HOUSE STYLE

JOHN FOWLER

THE INVENTION OF THE COUNTRY-HOUSE STYLE

EDITED BY

HELEN HUGHES

DONHEAD

Published with the assistance of the Getty Grant Program

Published by
Donhead Publishing Ltd
Lower Coombe, Donhead St Mary
Shaftesbury, Dorset SP7 9LY
Tel: +44(0)1747 828422
www.donhead.com

ISBN 1 873394 59 4

British Library Cataloguing in Publication Data

John Fowler: the invention of the country-house style
    1. Fowler, John, 1906– – Congresses 2. Historic buildings –
Conservation and restoration – Congresses 3. Interior
decoration – Congresses
I Hughes, Helen
721 ΄. 0288
ISBN 1873394594

Designed by Geoff Green Book Design
Printed in Sweden by
Kristianstad Book Printers Ltd

CONTENTS

ACKNOWLEGEMENTS

I MUST THANK ALL of the contributors to this publication as well as those involved in the organization of the two conferences 'Inspired by the Past: Kelmarsh Hall 1926–54' (19–20 November 1999, Kelmarsh Hall) and 'Inspired by the Past: John Fowler's approach to decoration and restoration in a changing world' (4 July 2001, London). The staff of the Kelmarsh Hall Estate Preservation Trust, particularly the late Cynthia Wright, the house manager, Peter Scott, the chairman of the Trust, and Edward Perry, the current house manager, along with George Ferguson and Marianne Suhr of Ferguson Mann Architects, were extremely supportive.

The Traditional Paint Forum conferences only come about due to the hard work and commitment of the committee members who from 1999 to 2001 included Una Richards, Peter Hood, Ian Bristow, Alan Gardner, Phillip Hartley, Richard Ireland, Patrick Baty, John Nevin, Paul Humphreys, John Stewart, Susanne Groome, Tina Sitwell and Keith Warwick.

Special thanks are due to Louise Henderson, Ian Crick, Michael Smith, John Richards, Tom Greening, and Frank Garbutt for all their help and support. The administration of the London conference was organized with great efficiency by Amanda Holgate. Maria Nyber-Coles and Colin Powel. I am grateful for the help and assistance provided by the staff and photographic libraries of *Country Life* and the National Trust and the archivists at Colefax & Fowler and Laura Ashley. I am grateful for additional information provided by Mario Buatta.

I am indebted to Tracy Manning who assisted in the editing of this book and sourcing the illustrations, John Stewart who managed the publication project, and the staff at Donhead for their advice and support. Full colour illustration has been made possible by a generous grant from the Getty Program.

AUTHOR BIOGRAPHIES

HELEN HUGHES, Head of Historic Interiors Research & Conservation English Heritage, and a founder member of the Traditional Paint Forum

SIR NEIL COSSONS, Chairman of English Heritage

PETER INSKIP, Director of Peter Inskip & Peter Jenkins Architects.

TIM KNOX, Head Curator, The National Trust

CHRISTINE SITWELL, Painting Conservation Advisor, The National Trust

PATRICK BATY, a consultant who advises on all aspects of decorative paint and colour and owner of a specialist London based paint business.

IAN BRISTOW, architect and specialist consultant in the redecoration of historic interiors

MARIANNE SÜHR, a Chartered Building Surveyor who works for the Society for the Preservation of Ancient Buildings (SPAB) as a technical promotions officer and as a self employed historic buildings consultant.

LOUISE WARD, a design historian awarded the first Oliver Ford Scholar at the Royal College of Art. Current research focuses on the professionalization of interior decoration and gender roles in post-war England.

FOREWORD

SIR NEIL COSSONS

CHAIRMAN OF ENGLISH HERITAGE

I T IS A TESTAMENT to John Fowler's career that more than twenty years after his death a day dedicated to a discussion of his work could generate so much interest. During the course of his long career John Fowler worked as an interior designer in some of Britain's most important historic buildings. His career spanned the pivotal post-Second World War period when there was a tremendous interest in renewing the country house and a great increase in visitor numbers.

Fowler drew his inspiration for his interior schemes from the past and devised a new style that was enormously popular. Using his innate good judgement and personal flair he created serene and subtle interiors that provided a wonderful background for great collections. He was ever anxious to avoid the 'dead hand of the restorer'. In these interiors nothing ever jarred and they were completely in keeping with the romantic taste of the period.

The papers included in this book discuss some of John Fowler's projects in detail but also broaden the discussion to include a consideration of how historic interiors were presented in the past and how we could be presenting them in the future. Of course the key to these issues is the acquisition of a full understanding of the history and development of these buildings. Without fully understanding Fowler's aims and objectives we cannot make a serious assessment of his work nor formulate policies for the future conservation of his extant schemes.

In his book on the work of John Fowler *The Inspiration of the Past*, published in 1985

(undeniably the most significant work to date on John Fowler), the architectural historian John Cornforth seemed to have anticipated these discussions. He predicted that in the future, 'when ... it becomes possible to look at the history of the country house in the twentieth century and see it in the perspective of the previous four centuries it will surely seem a surprising one'.[1] He wondered how we would view Fowler's schemes as decorations when they were no longer in pristine condition.

As we start the twenty-first century, how we understand and choose to present Fowler's comparatively recent decorative schemes may offer an opportunity to establish protocols for the treatment of all historic interiors. Decorative finishes, textiles, and architectural fittings are very vulnerable and are so easily lost or destroyed by well-meaning but over-zealous refurbishment. To this end English Heritage is working with UKIC (United Kingdom Institute for Conservation) to highlight the conservation problems facing these fragile areas within historic buildings.

Original Fowler schemes which have not been repainted or obliterated are becoming increasingly rare. What action should we be taking now? Is it better to retain the faded glory of his original work or redecorate to recapture the spirit of his intention? Have we the knowledge, skill, and materials to recreate the subtleties of the original scheme?

Fowler worked for private clients but his most accessible and familiar projects are those he carried out for the National Trust.

His work was also disseminated during his career through the illustrations of *Country Life*. The impact he had on his contemporaries was immense and long-lasting, so much so that today the 'Fowler style' has come to be considered by some as the only style for the decoration of a country house.

Fowler's work may be considered as a distinct period style of the mid-twentieth century, as yet another accretion to the evolving country house. Perhaps John Fowler's legacy is that he developed in his own period style something that reflected contemporary taste. We advocate the conservation and retention of historic schemes in some buildings and pursue accurate academic recreations in others; perhaps we should also be encouraging modern designers, as our predecessors have done for centuries.

The seeds for the conference were sown at an earlier gathering organized by the Traditional Paint Forum (TPF) at Kelmarsh Hall in November 1999. That event looked specifically at the work carried out there by John Fowler working in collaboration with the owner Nancy Lancaster. Fowler and Lancaster had a fruitful if turbulent professional relationship and were once described as 'the unhappiest unmarried couple in the world'.

Although the TPF is a small, newly formed society it has already established a reputation for organizing stimulating conferences and producing an interesting and informative journal. We are very happy to collaborate with them to present these papers and look forward to other joint ventures in the future.

References

1 Cornforth, John, *The Inspiration of the Past: Country House Taste in the Twentieth Century*, Viking, London, 1985, p. 9.

Introduction

✠

HELEN HUGHES

As well as discussing the work of John Fowler, this publication provides an overview of the conservation of historic interiors in the post-war period and a much-needed reappraisal of the development, or invention, of the 'country-house style'. Looking back, I realize that it was a request to investigate the existing decoration of the Entrance Hall of Kelmarsh Hall, near Market Harborough, that provided the initial inspiration which resulted in two conferences and the papers included in this volume.

The Entrance Hall at Kelmarsh – a grand double-height room designed by James Gibbs c.1728–32 – was believed to retain a scheme devised by John Fowler (1906–1977), 'doyen of English decorators for 25 years after the Second World War',[1] in collaboration with Nancy Lancaster (1897–1994), the sometime owner of Kelmarsh and also his business partner at Colefax & Fowler. The decorative finishes of the Entrance Hall seemed to be a wonderful example of Fowler's style and techniques. Unfortunately, the paint on the ceiling and walls was flaking badly and a decision had to be made as to whether the room should be redecorated or carefully conserved. The intriguing story of the investigation of the room highlights many of the problems of the conservation and representation of historic interiors (Sühr, pp. 52–8, Bristow, pp. 59–62).

This project prompted further interest in Nancy Lancaster's treatment of the other interiors at Kelmarsh and in her impact on country-house interiors in general. The result was a two-day conference and workshop held in November 1999 at Kelmarsh, entitled 'Inspired by the Past – Kelmarsh Hall 1926–1954', co-organized by the Traditional Paint Forum (TPF) and the Kelmarsh Preservation Trust. One of the great strengths of the Traditional Paint Forum is that it addresses both the ethical and technical issues surrounding historic-house conservation and presentation. As a unique umbrella group, it stimulates discussion and debate between a broad collection of building professionals, such as architectural historians, building analysts, architects, painters and decorators, and conservators. Since its foundation in 1994 the TPF has run a series of conferences which combine academic discussion and technical demonstrations, and it publishes a journal, *The Traditional Paint News*. The Kelmarsh Preservation Trust, founded in 1982, not only manages the Hall and the estate with great care and sensitivity, but provides access and training in the management and conservation of the natural and built heritage. It offers an excellent 'classroom' for heritage conservators, and runs a series of highly successful training seminars.

The Kelmarsh conference also included tours of the Hall and grounds, and technical demonstrations of painting techniques. We were fortunate to be joined by Jim Smart, Owen Turville, and Peter Hood who had worked with John Fowler, and Ken Cowens who had decorated the Entrance Hall in the 1950s. As an added bonus Jeff Orton demonstrated traditional plasterwork techniques *in situ* in the Ballroom where he was engaged on the recreation of ceiling and cornice. The two-day event was a great success, one of the most memorable highlights being a grand dinner held in the Entrance Hall itself, which, when decorated with flowers and with Fowler's delicate shades of pink illuminated by flickering candlelight and two roaring wood fires – and filled with convivial delegates – could claim to go some way to recreating 'the Nancy Lancaster experience'.

It was felt that the quality of the papers presented at this conference was such that they deserved a wider audience. With this in mind, the TPF in collaboration with English Heritage organized a one-day conference in London in July 2001 entitled 'Inspired by the Past – John Fowler's approach to decoration and restoration in a changing world', which focused its discussion more closely on the work of John Fowler. Of course a dark lecture theatre in London could not compete with the autumnal romance of Kelmarsh Hall, but it did have the advantage of offering a more central location and accommodating more delegates.

This second conference may be considered as a successor to John Cornforth's book *The Inspiration of the Past: Country House Taste in the Twentieth Century*, published in 1985, which was the last major assessment of John Fowler's work. Cornforth admitted that his book could not claim to provide a detached view of Fowler's work, since he was a close personal friend, and because Fowler had also been the co-author with him of a previous book, *English Decoration in the 18th Century* (Baty, pp. 31–40). The papers in this current volume, written almost twenty years after John Fowler's death, provide an overview of Fowler's work from several perspectives and reappraise his contribution in the light of new approaches to the study of historic interiors. The detailed analysis of Fowler's representation of the Saloon at Clandon (Inskip, pp. 1–12, Knox, pp. 13–20, Sitwell, pp. 21–30, Bristow, pp. 41–51) provides a fascinating insight into his working methods, and adds so much to our understanding of the room. The existing presentation of the room is not a recreation of the original eighteenth-century scheme – and

Fowler never intended it to be so – but a fusion of selected elements which reflected his own taste. To a certain extent, Fowler's transformation of so many of the National Trust's interiors did condition our perception of historic houses; with limited space for interpretation information, Fowler recreations were generally accepted by visitors as surviving historic schemes or careful recreations of such. The Fowler vision became the ubiquitous vision of the past, so much so that it became *de rigueur* for regional museum curators to paint all Georgian panelling in 'three shades of …'.

Today, Fowler's work is recognized as an example of the country-house style which evolved during the period 1930–1980 and, as such, deserves considered study and analysis – and careful conservation if his schemes are to be retained as a record of this significant historic style (Knox, pp. 13–20, Sitwell, pp. 21–30). Ian Bristow provides a review of the more academic approach to representation which was developing during the post-war period (Bristow, pp. 41–51). The modern-day building analyst and archaeologist is alarmed by references to Fowler's 'instinctive understanding', his 'excellent eye' and 'taste', and his selective use of historic evidence. But these scholars are rarely asked to engage with the practicalities of conservation and redecoration. It is easy to take the high ground – Ruskin declared 'Do not let us talk then of restoration. The thing is a lie from beginning to end.'[2] – and leave the project once the report stage has been completed. Historic-house curators, conservators, and decorators who have to wrestle with the physical and aesthetic practicalities may take a more understanding view of the problems that Fowler faced in many of the National Trust properties.

Fowler's contribution should be seen in the context of the period in which he was working. There is no right or wrong way to present a historic interior. Today we are acutely aware of the responsibility that we bear to future generations to gain an understanding of a building before we make any alterations, so as to ensure that we do not inadvertently destroy or obliterate significant elements or decorative finishes and that we retain archaeological evidence. But after these conditions have been observed, buildings are best preserved by being used and enjoyed. Our long-term responsibilities and the needs of the current users of the buildings are not mutually exclusive, and with skill and sensitivity they can be reconciled. Perhaps we should display more courage in commissioning modern designers to work within historic interiors. As long as there is honesty and clarity about how and why an interior is being presented in a particular manner, a wide range of conservation and representation solutions are often equally valid. Although the reconstruction of a period scheme may enhance a particular interior, in some cases it may be totally inappropriate. My visit after the conference to the Saloon at Clandon was enhanced by my new-found understanding of Fowler's 1968 recreation of the room: the nineteenth-century polychrome ceiling, the blue walls matched erroneously to the original undercoat layer, the black overmantel and white overpainted mahogany doors (complete inventions by Fowler), and the Second World War army-blanket curtains that he decided to retain. This is certainly not a reconstruction of an earlier decorative scheme, but it is an important scheme in its own right, and the National Trust is to be applauded for its intention of maintaining the room as a record of this period of the house's history.

The very idea of holding a conference to discuss Fowler's work was met with concern and even disapproval from several quarters. This is perhaps understandable, and it is indicative of the great loyalty and affection John Fowler inspired in his friends, colleagues, and clients. The more objective analysis of historic interiors that is now advocated,[3,4] based on the integration of documentary and archaeological investigation, may be seen to have been foreshadowed by Fowler's own attempts to establish the early decorative schemes in many of the buildings in which he worked. As Ian Bristow suggests, Fowler would certainly have utilized the more sophisticated methods of building investigation which are available today (Bristow, p. 49). The limitations of the traditional art-historical approach based solely on documentary sources and stylistic analysis are now well recognized. This collection of papers may be seen as something of a landmark in the use of multidisciplinary collaboration, where art historians and building analysts, conservators and craftsmen, demonstrate the benefits of pooling expertise to increase understanding of historic interiors. I hope these papers help establish a new methodology for the research of historic interiors. Collaborative research of this kind broadens the range of questions we can ask when studying historic buildings and will ultimately result in a more informed understanding of our past.

HELEN HUGHES
*Head of Historic Interiors Research &
Conservation, English Heritage
Events Organizer, The Traditional Paint
Forum (1995–2002)*

References

1 Cornforth, John, *The Inspiration of the Past: Country House Taste in the Twentieth Century*, Viking, London, 1985, p. 9.

2 Ruskin, J., 'The Lamp of Memory', *The Seven Books of Architecture*, (1st edition), 1849, p. 180.

3 Hughes, Helen (ed.), *Layers of Understanding: Setting Standards for Architectural Paint Research*, Donhead Publishing, Shaftesbury, 2002.

4 Clarke, Kate, *Informed Conservation*, English Heritage, London, 2001.

WORKING WITH JOHN FOWLER

PETER INSKIP

'OBSERVING JOHN FOWLER at work' would be more apposite as a title to this paper, and it is not intended to be more than that. I knew him when he was working on historic restorations for the National Trust. I did not know him earlier, when he was the successful society decorator creating fantasies in the Albany Chambers, Piccadilly for Mrs David Bruce and Pauline de Rothschild.[1] I watched him at work at Clandon Park and made drawings of details in Cambridge that he needed for Grimsthorpe. At Cornbury Park I was Philip Jebb's architectural assistant while John was decorating that great house, and later, at Newnham College, John helped with the decoration of the Hall when I was architect. Above all, John and I were great friends for the last twelve years of his life. Here, therefore, are some personal recollections; for a thorough analysis of his work, turn to *English Decoration in the 18th Century*, the book that John Cornforth wrote with John over many weekends at John's home, the Hunting Lodge in 1973,[2] and the same author's *The Inspiration of the Past: Country House Taste in the Twentieth Century* published in 1985.[3] Robert Becker's *Nancy Lancaster: Her Life, Her World, Her Art*[4] gives an understanding of the respective roles played by Mrs Lancaster and John Fowler in the firm of Colefax & Fowler before it changed and entered the world of big business in the years after John's death in 1977.

I met John Fowler when I was eighteen, in the early 1960s. The restoration of William Kent's No. 44 Berkeley Square had just been published in *Country Life*[5] and I had been on a visit to see it with the Georgian Group. John's restoration of the main rooms brought significance back to the house. It seemed very grand, but it appealed as it was also understated and above all it

Figure 1 The Staircase, No. 44 Berkeley Square post-Fowler. *Country Life Picture Library*

Figure 2 The Chapel, Cornbury Park. *Country Life Picture Library*

appeared to be scholarly. However, there was a concern that the introduction of a mirror in the recess on the half-landing of the staircase lost some of the drama of the staircase as the upper flight was now revealed too early. It was about the first of the restorations of the great London houses which had managed to survive the War, and I remember the Georgians combined their visit that day with a tour of *The Economist*'s office in a very run-down Spencer House, a building which was to wait nearly another 20 years for its restoration under Lord Rothschild.

John Fowler replied in his own fair hand to my enquiry in 1962 about the possibility of working for him while I waited to go up to Cambridge. It was a slightly prickly interview, but also very charming. He tested me on the date and provenance of some furniture that was in his room at the time. Fortuitously, I got the date of a chair right as 1790 and by accident I said it was British. He said that he liked my cautious approach,

as the piece was, of course, Scottish. I got offered a job if it was to be permanent, but I had to decline as I really wanted to go to university.

I came across him again when I was employed as an architectural assistant to Philip Jebb after I had graduated in 1965. The first visits with John to Cornbury while I was working for Philip involved very careful observation of the building, from Nicholas Stone's marvellous early work through to Hugh May's additions of the late seventeenth century and the enrichment of the house in the mid-eighteenth century. Belcher's overscaled Edwardian entrance was seen to detract terribly from the building and permission was granted to allow its removal, recovering the Chapel as a virtually free-standing building in the centre of a court. The Chapel is an outstanding work by Hugh May, but it reminded Lord Rotherwick, for whom John was working, of his school days and he was determined to demolish it. By the late sixties John was so confident in his position as the saviour of great houses that he threatened the owner with imprisonment if a finger was laid on the Chapel. He was also passionate about the Drawing Room and went to great pains to understand the detail of the extraordinary rococo architraves. This observation stage has to be seen as a key initial step in any of Fowler's restoration schemes.

In Cambridge, we worked together on the redecoration of the Hall at Newnham College. Fowler did not have a great interest in the architecture of the end of the nineteenth century, but Basil Champneys' design of 1884 was seen as good and its relationship to the garden made John enthusiastic. The key for the new decoration was to take a cue from the early eighteenth-century buildings that had inspired Champneys, rather than any thought of restoring the architect's very plain white scheme that had been implemented when it was built.

There were two architectural problems that needed to be resolved. The first was that, whilst the side and end walls were complex in the arrangement of the architectural decoration, the high-table end was extremely plain. The second was that the barrel-vaulted ceiling was isolated from the space below by the tie beams being set at such close centres that they 'read' as a ceiling at the very springing of the vault. Not only did the space contained by the vault need to be brought into play, but also the quality of the plasterwork deserved to be appreciated. Indeed, it was the best part of the design, being freely modelled by George Frampton,[6] who was later knighted and was famous for the statue of Peter Pan in Kensington Gardens put up in 1912.

To solve these problems, the scheme was to be an exercise in Fowler's famous 'three whites', which he felt provided a logical system for painting a room architecturally: the darkest white on the stiles and railings, the mid-white on the panels, and the lightest on the mouldings. Champneys' design, however, was not at all logical and the spandrel panels had to be painted another colour to differentiate them from the wall panelling. Above the cornice, the scheme rose into the vault, which was painted two lighter tones to allow for its being in the shade. The outstanding quality of Frampton's plasterwork was revealed by the two lightest whites, but additional emphasis was given by gilding. The disposition of this was worked out in stages, with one bay being marked out in yellow ochre as a trial. First, the cartouche and dates were highlighted, then their frames, then it was decided to gild the 'nail heads' to give a sparkle across the whole vault.

The colour chosen for the spandrels was a terracotta and this was continued at high level on the undecorated frieze above high table. The marvellous portraits by Sir James Shannon were to be cleaned and restored to their original position and hung on a grand large-scale damask-design wallpaper to give the richness that the end walls lacked. The effect reminded John of the pictures hung over the tapestries in the gallery at Hardwick Hall.

The fellows of the College were delighted with the proposal, especially as it established a hierarchy within the Hall that responded

Figure 3 Preliminary paint trials in the Hall at Newnham College.
Peter Inskip

to the high table. However, John did not think that the trial had worked. He felt that the scheme was too 'decoratory', that it 'looked as if a decorator had been there'. Something much calmer was required. An alternative was, therefore, developed with a very dark raw umber in place of the terracotta and a much simpler paper with a nineteenth-century trellis design on a plain ground restricted to the colours proposed for the panelling.

Trials in different areas of the room were carried out to judge the effect of different lighting conditions. Paint on a ceiling was made one or two shades lighter to adjust for the fact that it was always in shade. Gilding was by experiment and elements of the ceiling were painted in yellow ochre so that the effect could be reviewed from the ground; first just the cyphers and dates were touched in, then the borders and finally the diamond-shaped nail heads that punctuated each bay. The method was similar to the working out

Figure 4 (top) The Hall, Newnham College showing the finished scheme. *Peter Inskip*

Figure 5 (bottom) Exterior of Clandon showing the door leading into the Saloon. *National Trust Photographic Library*

at gaining the respect of the men and establishing a working relationship. The presence of new painters was recognized as a constraint and the scheme was intentionally simple at Newnham so that it could be realized by the College painters, Mr Bird and sons, who had not worked with John before. Trials were, therefore, important as a training exercise for those who were to implement a scheme. Of course, the painters would have the expected flat-oil, Walpamur water paint and pigments ready to hand, but we would stop en route at Ploton's shop in Highgate to buy raw umber, and black seemed to be inevitably used in most colours to give them 'weight'. Mixing was the first test for the painters, but it was also one where John allied with them by taking part in the process himself. Mr Bird and his sons were totally unaware that their work was being discussed discreetly when John referred to the 'Oiseaux'.

My frequent visits to Clandon did not have any professional basis on my part, but came about as John could not drive. An invitation to stay with him for the weekend, therefore, meant providing a taxi service on Friday to take him to see progress on his jobs on the way to his cottage at Odiham. It was a marvellous part-time apprenticeship.

At Clandon, the main rooms were being repaired and re-presented by the National Trust. John's first visits were concerned with understanding the use of the house. Looking and thinking not only about the rooms, but how the house was originally used, he would consider how each space fitted into the hierarchy of the building, especially when it was used as a house of parade. Of course, there was always a hunt for any black paint over gilding on furniture, picture frames, and looking glasses as John was obsessed with funeral traditions and discovering evidence of mourning.

The progress from the double-height white-painted Hall to the Saloon was an anticlimax in the 1960s, with the latter not only used as a sitting room but also decorated to match the Hall. In contrast with the double-height Hall, the Saloon only fills one storey and at the time both were white

of the gilding on the gates at Clandon and at Fenton House, Hampstead, that John had recently completed for the National Trust. One understood the logic of the design and then brought it forward in stages, ensuring that the balance was maintained all the time.

There was also the question of working with a new contractor and John was wonderful

Figure 6 The Saloon, Clandon, 1927. *Country Life Picture Library*

rooms. However, the panelling had been covered for many years with wallpaper possibly similar to the Amberley pattern found in several rooms in the house. Paint scrapes carried out with spatulas revealed that 'originally' a strong contrast between the two rooms was effected through the use of colour, with whites in the Hall giving way to rich blues, black, and biscuit in the Saloon. Paint scrapes were not a new idea and indeed John said that Nancy Lancaster had done them at Ditchley in the 1930s; and certainly at Haseley, thirty years later, she was busy scraping away with a threepenny piece to see what the original colours were and how she could use them to 'inspire' a new scheme. However, in the late 1960s the 'restoration' projects that Fowler was taking on for the National Trust allowed a different slant and there was a real interest in recovering the way a room had been originally decorated.

John's first scrapes at Clandon revealed the range of colours of an earlier scheme – the pale blue ground, the pale biscuit ground to the medallions, and the stone-white colour of the ornament. When it was decided

to proceed with the scheme it proved possible to remove the overlying distemper to expose virtually all of the colours he had discovered. (Sitwell, p. 29, Figure 9) The walls, however, had been repainted with oil, rather than soft distemper, and could not be cleaned down. Fragments of the palest and darkest blue were left exposed, therefore, to show how closely the modern restoration followed the original. One carry-over from the concept of the three whites was that the middle blue on the stiles and rails was chosen as being halfway between them rather than being based on evidence. The skirting was also painted a blueberry-black according to what John described as Palladian custom, as that was what he expected. It would be interesting to examine these details with paint microscopy. That is not a criticism: Fowler's scheme was a big step forward for the time, but it is now over thirty years ago and things are much advanced.

As with the ceiling, all the colours in the entablature after cleaning were seen by John and the National Trust as original and only needed touching up. The modillion cornice

Figure 7 The Saloon, Clandon, post-Fowler. *National Trust Photographic Library*

was in two tones of biscuit and stone, with red used as a ground to the paterae, while the stone-coloured ornament in the frieze was on a blue ground. The door-cases and dado rail were painted in two tones of biscuit by John, following scrapes, and the mahogany doors, that were later introductions, were painted in a third, paler, biscuit and two tones of white. In photographs of 1927 the whole of the chimney piece appeared dark, but when the room was whitened the plaster overmantle was washed over too. Fowler marbleized it to match the *porto venere* marble of the chimney piece and the central relief was painted to follow the white marble frieze of the chimney piece and make it resemble the reliefs by the eighteenth-century sculptor Michael Rysbrack in the Hall. As *Country Life* said at the time:[7]

> ... the discovery of this scheme is a fascinating one, because we have little information about the way rich plasterwork was treated in the pre-Adam period.

The redecoration was seen to underline the true character of the space as a room of parade, and the recovery of a formal arrangement of furniture around the walls was integral to the scheme. John Cornforth described the approach to the restoration of Clandon as:[8]

> ... empirical, for it is influenced by such a variety of considerations, visual and comparative evidence, historical style and sentiment, the need to create a unity where there may be elements of different dates to be absorbed.

Wallpapers were also uncovered at Clandon. One case was in the Green Drawing Room, which had been hung with a yellow silk damask since the nineteenth century – a nice survival of a name despite the room changing its colour. When the walling was taken down a green paper was revealed. Printed with the Amberley pattern on small sheets, approximately 20 × 22 inches, it was rather crudely put up, apparently when the room was first decorated since it extended behind the overmantle that was probably introduced sometime after 1740. The paper was taken down for conservation, rebacked and then lightly sized as it had been varnished sometime in the past and was seen in 1967 as unpleasantly shiny. It was rehung in a slightly higgledy-piggledy fashion to maintain its original appearance and supplemented in missing areas by the paper discovered behind the overmantle – a disturbance of evidence that I don't think we would consider today. The gilding of the overmantle was retained, but that on the dado and doorcase could not be recovered and was redone. The gilding of the entablature was another survival except for the top fillet to the cornice, which was gilded by John 'to increase the sense of definition between the wall and ceiling'.[9] At the same time, he whitened the ribbons of the pulvinated frieze.

One alteration that John contemplated was the painting of a bust in the Hall – because of its slightly Negroid features – as a blackamoor, especially as this would have reflected the Cranleys' connections with the West Indies. However, this was not implemented out of deference to the feelings of one of the team of painters, who was black. Again, today paint analysis would solve such problems.

Once we got to the Hunting Lodge at Odiham, we entered a miniature world of all that John admired in the great houses he worked on. Acquired as a derelict cottage in 1947, it changed very little over the years – once the garden, with its lawns and clipped hornbeam hedges, had been made. It was this garden that convinced Sir Hardy Amies, the Queen's dressmaker, that when he bought a country cottage, it should have neither lawn nor hedges so that he might have time to enjoy the place when he was there.[10] The Hunting Lodge had been constructed as a Gothic eye-catcher in the middle of the eighteenth century, and was very small. It was simply decorated but some elements were of a large scale, and Marie-Antoinette's gloves hanging on heroic Maunay wallpaper demonstrated what John called 'peasantry grandeur'.

Saturdays would be given over to gardening. John loved burning leaves in the autumn and on occasion I would be given the daunting task of cutting the Portuguese laurels which had been given to him by Nancy Lancaster – who had originally acquired them for Ditchley when the gardens at Wrest Park were sold up. Other guests, however, managed to avoid gardening and John Cornforth would busy himself with the next chapter of *English Decoration*, which he was

Figure 8 (top) The Green Drawing Room, Clandon, hung with yellow silk damask, 1969. *Country Life Picture Library*

Figure 9 (bottom) The Green Drawing Room, Clandon, post-Fowler. *Country Life Picture Library*

Figure 10 (left) Jim Smart and his team of painters, who carried out the work at Clandon. *Peter Inskip*

Figure 11 (right) The Hunting Lodge, Odiham. *Peter Inskip*

then writing with John. Dinner was always very enjoyable on Saturday, even if Fowler believed that the champagne should be warm. Jim Lees-Milne and Eardley Knowles of the National Trust came frequently, and John's neighbour, Rachel Redgrave, was inevitably there on Saturday or Sunday. Occasionally, a special treat would be dinner at Hackwood with Princess Joan Ally Kahn. There was a lot of television on Sunday night.

Weekends sometimes meant a visit to Haseley Court to see Nancy Lancaster. It was the most remarkable house, and represented the best of both of them. It was here

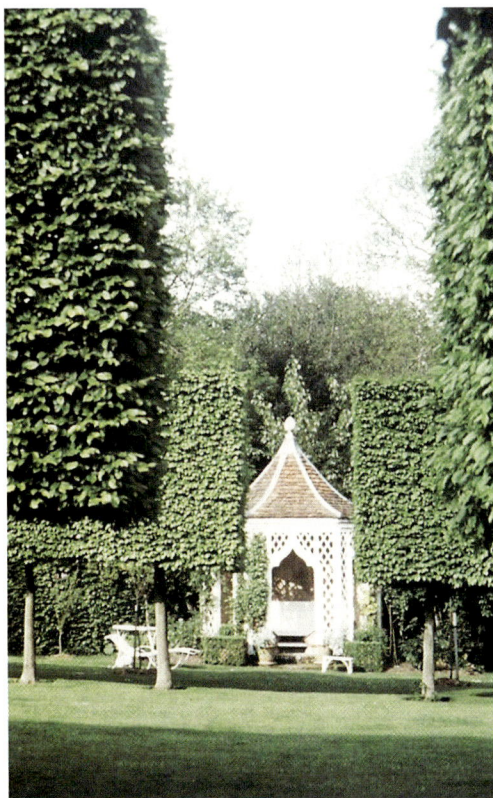

Figure 12 The Summer House at the Hunting Lodge, Odiham. *Peter Inskip*

that John returned to his role of actual painter, recalling his painting of Chinese wallpapers in the 1930s. With George Oakes he made such a paper for the Palladio Room, and together they also painted the *trompe l'oeil* decoration of the bedroom occupied by Nancy's aunt, the formidable Lady Astor. Both John and Mrs Lancaster were passionate gardeners and the garden at Haseley, based on Virginian precedents, was heavily influenced by John's own garden at the Hunting Lodge as well as by Villandry in France, about which everybody was enthusiastic at the time.

But there was also a very serious side to these weekends. One was very conscious that John was thinking out problems and he would debate with his guests how the decoration of the houses he was working on should be approached. Trophies in the form of a piece of wallpaper, a chair, or casket would have been borrowed from the property to inspire him (they were always carefully returned), and these objects and decorative artefacts would be assembled to guide the resolution of problems.

John would also fantasize about how things came about. The fact that the fragment of the sprig wallpaper at No. 44 Berkeley Square was found used upside down was seen as evidence that it was older than the house and that it had been used up as a lining paper in the 1740s. From this, he deduced that the pattern would have been rather out of date when the house was built and he felt that the diagonal grid gave a quilted effect that really was of the seventeenth century rather than the eighteenth. It was clear to him that a delicately painted chair of the 1790s, which he discovered completely covered in black horsehair, had been modified with a head rest when it had been relegated to the servants' quarters and adopted as the favourite place for an aged butler to sleep.[11]

John would discuss current work at Ramsbury, Christ Church, and Wallington. Paint scrapes combined with careful observation assured him that he had found the authentic scheme and, of course, English Heritage had missed the point in its redecoration of Chiswick, where rumour had it that the decoration of the Lower Tribune (or hall) had studiously reproduced the primer rather than the final coat. There was very little, if any, archival research, but again, what he was doing at the time has to be seen as progressive. Documentary research in relation to colour and the use of microscopic analysis had not yet been adopted from the studio of the picture restorer as possible tools in determining historic decoration.

Establishing the original decorative scheme of a room was seen as essential, but at the same time it was felt that there was no reason that it should be slavishly reconstructed. I would be surprised if paint analysis showed that the library at Christ Church, with its wonderful plasterwork by Thomas Roberts, was other than white when it was originally decorated, but John domesticated it with a terracotta scheme with stone-white ornament. In the Saloon at Wallington, he was convinced that reversing the white decoration on the blue ground that he had found on the walls to blue on white would restore a balance, whilst he left the ceiling and cove untouched. Balance was determined by a response to the ageing of a house, its contents, and use. Choice was an acceptable step in the 1960s as long as it was somehow informed by what had gone before, but how this might be compromising authenticity was not recognized at the time.

John worked occasionally at Waddesdon Manor and Eythrope for Mrs James de Rothschild. He found it exciting when the Rothschilds approached him about moving out of Waddesdon, as the National Trust

Figure 13 Haseley Court. *Peter Inskip*

Figure 14 Berkeley sprig paper. *Peter Inskip*

was to take over the big house, and they were to move into the Pavilion at Eythrope at the other end of the estate, adopting this as their permanent home. He asked Mrs de Rothschild if she had some nice things to go in her new home and he recalled that with a twinkle in her eye she replied 'the best'. As well as the recasting of the Pavilion that the architect George Devey had designed for Miss Alice de Rothschild, rooms were also redone

Figure 15 Ditchley colour sample. *Peter Inskip*

at the Manor. There, bedrooms were opened up to form the Long Gallery to display costumes and drawings, or redecorated to become the Pastimes Room. In the anteroom to the dining room, Fowler marbleized a corner cupboard that he designed for displaying Meissen porcelain, and Mrs de Rothschild asked him to sign and date his work.

However, John's efforts at Waddesdon were sadly disappointing. I remember him looking back on this work and being frustrated as he felt the scheme was compromised. Whilst the Rothschild collections were seen as outstanding in the 1950s, few people fully appreciated the quality of the late nineteenth-century building at that time and the approach taken ended in a mixture of English country house and French tastes. In retrospect, Fowler regretted that they had not taken the opportunity to respond fully to the great nineteenth-century interiors with their superb hangings and fringes. Mrs de Rothschild was never aware of the way he felt and, when I was asked to start work on my own account at Waddesdon in 1984, she

would always tell me how devoted she and her companion, Miss Brassey, were to John. Since her death nearly all traces of his work at the Manor have been removed, but the signed corner cupboard does remain in store. Knowing his views about the work at Waddesdon, I do not think he would have minded its loss too much.

I know, however, that he did get saddened by the transience of decoration, since it was the first item subject to change should there be a divorce or death in a family. That was one of the reasons he liked working for the National Trust as he felt that his work had a better chance of survival.

He would also discuss the schemes he was proudest of where he had avoided redecoration. Lord Bagot had been warned that Mr Fowler could be very expensive, but John loved recounting how when he had arrived at Blithfield, he had just asked for a bucket of water and a scrubbing brush and had washed off the grey distemper from the walls of the hall to reveal the early nineteenth-century painting marked out as faux blocks of ashlar. Uppark was also a prized house because of the survival, before the fire, of such rare finishes, from its bleached floors, scrubbed with beer, to its early untouched eighteenth-century paints and gilding. Sometimes, a weekend jaunt would be to see original fabrics and early paint at The Vyne, nearby at Basingstoke; on another occasion I took him over to Ampthill in Bedfordshire to see Avenue House, a building largely untouched since 1919 when it was acquired and decorated by Albert Richardson, later President of the Royal Academy.

Application was equally as important as the colour. Fowler loved and could use original techniques and knew what could be achieved with various natural pigments. But these were also important when the intention was not just to reproduce a historic colour, but also to recreate the quality and effect that John and Nancy Lancaster had observed in rooms where old paint actually survived. It was a painterly approach and it was a theatrical approach. Stippling and dragging were often a means to this end, and a colour would be dependent on one colour being seen through another, as was the case at Boughton where a dragged blue–grey was enlivened by a crimson ground. Where colours were based on scrapes, he would produce a record of his interpretation of the original colour, such as the example he gave me of the original decoration in the Breakfast Room at Ditchley. He thought it a very 'grand' colour.

John had decorated Folly Farm for Mrs Astor, but he had little interest in Lutyens and, as was the case with his response to Champneys at Newnham, was much more passionate about the buildings of the early eighteenth century that might have inspired the architect in its design. The decoration, therefore, followed the Colefax & Fowler English country-house style and in those terms was a success. One weekend, I remember a letter arriving completely out of the blue from Mrs Astor which went something on the lines of:

> Folly darling [as he was always called by the set focused on Nancy Lancaster], I am sitting in the drawing room which you helped us with so many years ago. The pink has now faded to a complete nothingness. Today, it is looking so wonderful that I just had to write and tell you. Love …

Behind that paint lay Lutyens's black walls with pure white detail relieved only by Chinese red on a balcony railing.

The search for the perfect pink continued up to his death. One weekend at the Hunting Lodge, John asked me to paint the walls of the tiny kitchen that had just been built to serve his garden pavilion. The walls were pristine white and I was told to paint them with a terracotta wash 'as loosely and as roughly as possible'. When it was finished, John's comment was, 'It is lovely, but I will ask Stanley Falconer [one of his colleagues at 'the Shop'] to repaint it when he comes to stay next weekend'. I do not think it ever was repainted, and the effect was copied and used many times elsewhere.

I believe that the use of his famous three whites was also part of this syndrome of

Figure 16 John Fowler at the Hunting Lodge. *Gervaise Jackson Stops*

achieving the look of ancient paintwork. Although there might be some evidence of different colours and shades used in the eighteenth century in order to allow an architectural interpretation of a room, today we know that there was nothing like as much as John imagined and that usually colours were painted solid and not picked out. We have to take it that in reality John's approach appears to have been a romantic one, to give the illusion of old painted schemes. Hardy Amies, a devoted friend of John's for over fifty years, always asked him to help when his salon in Savile Row required redecorating:[12]

> When John was alive there was no question of having anything other than three whites whenever it was due for repainting, but once he was dead, we just painted it white. Having it three whites, you know, never sold another frock.

References

1 See Cornforth, John, *The Inspiration of the Past: Country House Taste in the Twentieth Century*, Viking, London, 1985; and Jones, Chester, *Colefax and Fowler: The Best in English Interior Decoration*, Barrie & Jenkins, London, 1989.

2 Fowler, John and Cornforth, John, *English Decoration in the 18th Century*, Barrie & Jenkins, London, 1974.

3 Cornforth, John, *op. cit.* 1985.

4 Becker, Robert, *Nancy Lancaster: Her Life, Her World, Her Art*, Alfred A. Knopf, New York, 1996.

5 *Country Life*, vol. cxxxii, p. 1648.

6 The work is signed and dated in the plasterwork.

7 *Country Life*, vol. cxlvi, pp. 1456, 1582.

8 Ibid.

9 Ibid.

10 Recollection by Sir Hardy Amies to the writer about his garden at the Old School, Langford, Gloucestershire, 2000.

11 Sold to Humphrey Whitbread and now at Southill, Bedfordshire.

12 Recollection by Sir Hardy Amies to the writer, 2000.

JOHN FOWLER AND THE NATIONAL TRUST

TIM KNOX

JOHN CORNFORTH, writing in *The Inspiration of the Past* in 1985, stated that:[1]

> Posterity will learn of John Fowler's work largely through what he did for the National Trust in the last twenty years of his life … it is likely that the rooms he restored and decorated in the Trust's houses will be valued at least in part for his interpretation of them and will be preserved partly because of that.

Indeed, Fowler's work for the National Trust houses is now perhaps the best-known and most accessible part of his oeuvre, owing to the fact that many of his decors for private clients have been expunged by changes in ownership and fashion. However, as John Cornforth points out, Fowler's work for the Trust and private clients differed greatly and this paper – which is merely a pendant to the chapter in John's book entitled 'John Fowler's Contribution to the National Trust' – will discuss Fowler's work for the Trust and attempt to identify its principal characteristics.[2] I also want to touch upon the implications of the Trust's preservation – or replacement – of its Fowler decors.

It was James Lees-Milne, the National Trust's first Historic Buildings Secretary, who introduced John Fowler to the Trust in the 1950s. He had been introduced to him in March 1944 by the antique dealer and decorator Geoffrey Houghton-Brown.[3] Lees-Milne himself later wrote in *People and Places*:[4]

> At all events I can claim the credit of introducing John Fowler to the Trust in the 1950s. This scholarly decorator, with his sure sense

of history, was to leave an indelible imprint upon many interiors of our grandest country houses.

Fowler's first Trust commission was Claydon House in Buckinghamshire. When the National Trust was given Claydon in 1956 the house was in a deplorable state. It had been used as a girls' school during the War and a big sale in 1954 had stripped it of most of its – mainly Victorian – furniture. Sir Ralph Verney, who gave the house to the Trust, recalls the upper rooms being filled with tin baths to catch water from the leaking roofs, 'while little worm casts littered the floor in the Chinese Room'.[5] After the roof and repairs had been tackled by Hugh Creighton, John Fowler, a historically minded decorator to the 'living' private country houses, was called upon to advise on improvements to the interior decoration of the staterooms. The redecoration was financed from a grant from the Historic Buildings Council. Fowler was very busy at this period with Colefax & Fowler, so he rarely went to the house after the initial consultation. As Fowler mostly gave his services free to the Trust, he could hardly be expected to give the sort of constant attendance which his opulent private clients paid for, but boards painted with the suggested colours were sent up from London and the work was carried out under the direction of Christopher Wall, the Trust's Historic Buildings Representative.[6] Years later, in 1976, Fowler was consulted again over Claydon. The paint used in the 1956–7 redecoration had been of poor quality and was flaking badly, and an anonymous private

benefactor stepped in with the funds to redo it. The £25,000 enabled Fowler to have the work done by his own craftsmen, again under Christopher Wall's supervision. Although he was increasingly incapacitated by ill health by this time, it is interesting to see how Fowler amended his own original schemes second time round.

Most of Fowler's schemes survive intact at Claydon, bar a periodic refreshing of the white woodwork. Perhaps his most successful room is the North Hall, the walls of which he painted a pale ochreso as to contrast with the virtuoso white-painted woodwork designed by Luke Lightfoot (*c.* 1722–89). The ceiling is picked out in shades of lemon, white, and a pale pistachio green. Originally the insides of the niches were painted a dark, shiny green, but this was changed in 1976 to the pale green used on the ceiling. There were endless attempts to furnish the niches properly, with Chinese vases, lamps, and even gilded polychrome blackamoors sent over from Dorneywood where it was feared they

Figure 3 (left) The Chinese Room, Claydon, c.1956–7. *National Trust Photographic Library*

Figure 4 (right) The Chinese Room, Claydon, 1979–80. *National Trust Photographic Library*

would embarrass visiting African dignitaries. The niches are now occupied by a superb set of marble busts representing the Continents, just as described in the 1784 sale catalogue of the 2nd Earl Verney's effects, but otherwise the North Hall is as Fowler left it after his second visitation. It is in no sense a historic scheme, but it is tremendously successful nonetheless.

Next door, in the Saloon, Fowler hung a blue flock wallpaper, reinstating what was probably its original wallcovering. Nothing survived of the original, so Fowler copied a favourite eighteenth-century paper of this type he had found at Lydiard Tregoze in Wiltshire, printing it in the required colourway. By 1976 its colour had flown to a dirty grey and it was simply revived by spraying with blue paint. In the Staircase Hall, the ornaments of Joseph Rose's neoclassical plasterwork were picked out with white, on blue grounds, against walls of a pinkish biscuit colour. This was not a historical scheme but one borne out of a desire to make the most of the filigree plasterwork, once painted a uniform white. However, the balustrade of the staircase itself was the subject of careful paint scrapes and was put back to what John Fowler believed to be its original livery of black and gold – much to the annoyance of the Verney family, who

staunchly maintained that the 2nd Earl Verney, who built Claydon, had abhorred gilding and forbade its use anywhere in the house. Upstairs, the Chinese Room was at first painted yellow and pink, with white woodwork, the colours of the room from the mid-nineteenth century.[7] But on his second visit, Fowler repainted the walls all blue, presumably on the basis of paint scrapes. Recent paint analysis has confirmed his findings, and Fowler's match is remarkably close to the original eighteenth-century colour.[8] The sulphur-yellow silk curtains and divan were made to Fowler's specifications too. He also chose the wallpaper in Florence Nightingale's Room and it was probably he who preserved the Victorian pale-oak graining on the woodwork there – for he was usually respectful of such survivals, whatever their date, providing they were well done.

Clandon Park in Surrey was another of the Trust's gaunt, largely empty houses, and John Fowler was called in to redecorate it as a setting for Mrs Hannah Gubbay's distinguished collection of English furniture and porcelain, a non-indigenous collection that had been bequeathed in 1969.[9] Mrs Gubbay's money, and a gift from Mr and Mrs Kenneth Levy, enabled the house to be put in order, so funds weren't as tight at Clandon as at Fowler's other National Trust commissions – although eventually corners had to be cut even here over quality of materials. Here Fowler worked with St John Gore, then the regional Historic Buildings Representative, and John Cornforth advised on aspects of the interior decoration. As at Claydon, Fowler's work at Clandon plays up the magnificent architecture and decorative plasterwork of

Figure 5 The Saloon, Uppark, early paintwork retained by Fowler. *National Trust Photographic Library*

the house, sometimes according to historical precedent and sometimes not, but the overall idea was to emphasize the eighteenth-century elements in the house and remove what were seen as dowdy and ugly nineteenth-century incursions.

I won't go into much detail over John Fowler's work at Clandon – Tina Sitwell will do this in the next paper – but I want to look briefly at his transformation of the Saloon because it shows him struggling to reconcile the historical evidence he found with his desire to create a visually successful room (Inskip pp. 4–7, Figures 6, 7; Sitwell pp. 27–30, Figures 6, 7, 8, 9). The key to the room was its rich plasterwork ceiling which, when freed from layers of distemper, was found to be picked out with colourful polychromy – which Fowler believed to be from the eighteenth century but which has since

been discovered to date from 1879. Fowler kept this colouring and painted the walls in three tones of blue to match, on the evidence of scrapes. On the same basis, the overmantel above the ponderous black and white marble chimney piece was transformed into a funereal confection of almost Sicilian boldness and drama. Yet he also – for John Fowler had a sense of humour as well as of style and history – chose to retain the curtains made out of dyed American army blankets in the 1940s. But one senses that Fowler was uneasy about this room and struggled to justify and harmonize its disparate elements. It is known, for instance, that he elaborated the formerly simple allocation of black and white on the overmantel to make it look less oppressive and, in a talk he gave at Clandon in November 1968, Fowler conceded that the dark blue of the walls was 'a very surprising colour', suggesting that an alternative biscuit colour also found might be tried 'to see which would look best'.[10] The resultant room was much criticized even at the time – even Lees-Milne uncharitably wrote of it in *Ancient as the Hills* (1979): 'looking round, I thought it the most hideous decoration I had seen: flesh pink (which John Fowler calls biscuit) and purple [sic]'.[11]

But Fowler was quite prepared to alter or obliterate historical evidence if it didn't fit in with his plans. In the Green Drawing Room at Clandon a precariously preserved brocatelle (now thought to be pre-1778) was removed from the walls to reveal the original green flock wallpaper underneath (Inskip pp. 6–7, Figures 8, 9). When cleaned, the pale ground of this paper was thought to be too contrasting and its original lustrous sheen unattractive, so it was laboriously toned down.[12] One senses that Fowler disliked shininess or dominant patterns, and a characteristic of his interiors is their matt surfaces and his liking for expanses of plain colour or small-scale repetitive pattern, which ties in with his sparse, monumental placement of furnishings. He was certainly appalled by a lively red and gold flock paper put up by the Trust in the Edwardian Saloon at Stourhead, telling Lees-Milne (who had

Figure 6 (left) The Staircase, Sudbury Hall, pre-Fowler, c.1935. *National Trust Photographic Library*

Figure 7 (right) The Staircase, Sudbury Hall, post-Fowler. *National Trust Photographic Library*

ordered it) 'Laddie, it is what you would expect to find in the Bewdlay-House pipe shop'.[13] Some rooms at Clandon were redecorated entirely anew, with little or no reference to their historical appearance. In the Hunting Room the indigenous tapestries were hung against a foil of dark ochre-coloured textile with a diaper of little lozenges – a sort of ticking greatly favoured by John Fowler, who claimed that it was the material used to line carriages in the eighteenth century. A fitted carpet in complementary colours was laid on the floor, its trellis motif and border adapted from a Regency carpet at Tatton Park in Cheshire rather than anything at Clandon. But for all these historicist touches the resultant room is unmistakeably of its time – the late 1960s – particularly the tremendous billowing festoon blinds over the windows, made up from that squiggly moss-pattern chintz Fowler used so extensively in private practice. These curtains were to cause consternation at the 1986 National Trust Arts Panel visit to Clandon, when Sir Brinsley Ford was moved to observe that they 'were distinctly reminiscent of housemaid's knickers'.[14] Yet it was this Arts Panel which endorsed the

decision to keep the John Fowler decors at Clandon intact. Clandon remains, therefore, with the possible exception of Sudbury, the most extensive and best-preserved example of a Fowler-decorated house in Trust ownership.

My last example of John Fowler's work for the Trust is Sudbury Hall in Derbyshire, yet another architecturally distinguished but sparsely furnished house, which he did up on a shoestring budget.[15] This was one of Fowler's most successful interventions but it was also the scene of the stormiest protests. In June 1971, John Cornforth wrote the newly decorated house up in *Country Life*.[16] His thoughtful article carefully charted Fowler's interventions, describing the problems the Trust faced presenting it to the public. The article covered the conservative treatment of the two great rooms, the Saloon and the Long Gallery, noting that their nineteenth-century white and grey paintwork had merely been washed (a practice Fowler constantly championed, most notably at Uppark) or refreshed, the ceilings being picked out in three shades of soft white distemper to accentuate the sumptuous relief of the Carolean plasterwork. But the great innovation, the Staircase – its walls, which had been painted cream, painted the now-famous 'Sudbury Yellow', with the carved stair itself stripped of its sticky-looking Victorian dark varnish and painted two shades of white – was swiftly passed over in a sentence. Retribution came, in the form of a letter to *Country Life* from Lord Vernon, whose family had owned Sudbury until its transfer to the National Trust via the Treasury in 1963.

Vernon, who claimed he had never been consulted at any stage during the restoration, conceded that 'certain attractive innovations [had] been made' to the decoration of his ancestral seat, but complained of 'the deliberate change which [had] been wrought in the character and personality of the house'.[17] His Lordship's main criticism was the white Staircase. There was no evidence, he asserted, that it had originally been this colour, the traces of white paint found on it were the result of a disastrous misunderstanding with a nineteenth-century agent. The National Trust defended its scheme, saying that the white colour was indeed early – and was not the Staircase at Coleshill painted white also?[18] Both sides took up cudgels – Robin Fedden and John Cornforth for the Trust and Fowler, a host of others for Lord Vernon. One of the latter, Richard Tyler, wrote in August 1971 of how the Staircase had 'been unsexed' and prettified. 'Many of us are familiar with, and admire, the considerable talents of Mr John Fowler, the Trust's decorator, and his experts,' he wrote:[19]

> … but his very recognisable taste is what now dominates Sudbury. The clock has not been turned back to 1671: it has been set to '1971: Period of National Trust Redecoration'.

The row at Sudbury eventually subsided and Fowler's Staircase has now passed into the canon of twentieth-century country-house decoration, but I think we were taught an important lesson. The National Trust, a guardian of historic-house museums, not living family houses, should not perhaps have permitted a decorator to impose his taste upon them in a way that a private proprietor might do. The wholesale redecoration of Trust houses by John Fowler between 1956 and 1971 may well have made them look more presentable, but did nothing for their individuality or family atmosphere. As Pamela, Countess of Onslow, wrote in an elegiac article entitled 'Clandon Park: a House that was once a Home', published in 1971:[20]

> Now it has become a museum: a perfect period house, recreated by one of England's better-known interior decorators, who, with careful rapture and apparently inexhaustible funds, has restored and utterly transformed a Palladian palace … but it may be of interest to posterity to know that before Clandon Park took on its splendid new look a real family occupied a real house – a family whose possessions included late Victorian furniture and who positively liked not very nice Indian rugs, Benares brass ornaments, stuffed birds and dreadful photographs of babies, and who used door stops made from favourite horses' hooves.

But in defence of Fowler and the National Trust, what else could they do? The houses Fowler transformed were almost all empty and neglected, and bore the marks of the hard usage to which they had been put during the War.[21] At his most successful John Fowler revitalized drab rooms and emphasized the architecture and decoration in those which were inadequately furnished. Moreover, he was far more knowledgeable and historically sensitive than any of his contemporaries, and he did consult documents when they were made available to him. Paint analysis was also done – pioneering work with threepenny bits – and his many gifts of interesting fragments of historic textiles and wallpapers to the study collections of the Victoria & Albert Museum attest to his encyclopaedic understanding of the subject.[22]

In any case, there is much to admire in his bold and revelatory approach, and one sometimes longs for the flair and confidence of Fowler when encountering some of the unimaginative, slavishly 'correct' restorations that go on today. What is clear, moreover, is that the interiors he created for the Trust are now beginning to have their own period charm and significance in the history of country-house taste. I am not suggesting that every Fowler decor is reverently left as it is – his interventions at houses like Wallington, Montacute, or Lyme seem unsympathetic and at odds with the character of those places, and probably deserve to be reconsidered.[23] Nor should what I call 'Son of Fowler' schemes – those carried out by others, not under his general supervision, or those merely inspired by his distinctive taste – be sacrosanct.[24] But John Fowler's most successful transformations, Sudbury, Clandon, and Claydon – all houses with a strong architectural character but little indigenous 'kit' – should surely be left as they are.[25] After all, how else would one present them? Although they may be out of key with present-day taste and thinking, we should consider very carefully before we obliterate Fowler's most significant interiors beneath reinstated graining and 'authentic paint'. In this context it is worth recalling that the Duchess of Devonshire – who knows a thing or two about country houses and was on the committee advising on the decoration of Sudbury – called him the 'prince of decorators, a scholar with a wonderful memory for whole rooms and the smallest details … the best appreciator of beautiful places and things I have ever known'.[26]

References

1 Cornforth, John, *The Inspiration of the Past: Country House Taste in the Twentieth Century*, Viking, London, 1985, p. 200.
2 Ibid., pp. 200–21.
3 John Fowler for the first time and described him as 'a very sympathetic man'. Lees-Milne, James, *Prophesying Peace*, London, Chatto & Windus, 1977, pp. 33–4.
4 Lees-Milne, James, *People and Places: Country House Donors and the National Trust*, Murray, London, 1992, p. 17.
5 *Claydon House*, National Trust guidebook, 1999, pp. 4–6.
6 I am grateful to Christopher Wall for discussing with me his work with John Fowler at Claydon. Anthea Palmer and Hugo Brown have also kindly checked the Claydon files at Hughenden Manor for material relating to Fowler's work in the house.
7 Slides showing this pink and yellow scheme are preserved in the National Trust Historic Buildings Departmental archive.
8 Carried out by Jane Waddington in 2001, see her *Report* in the archives of the National Trust Thames and Chilterns Regional Office at Hughenden Manor, Buckinghamshire.
9 Guidebook, 2001. I am grateful to Christopher Rowell and Sophie Chessum for discussing with me John Fowler's work at Clandon.
10 Typescript 'Notes on a talk given by Mr John Fowler at Clandon on Wednesday 6th November 1968' in the archives of the National Trust Southern Region at Polesden Lacy.
11 Lees-Milne, James, *Ancient as the Hills: diaries 1973–1974*, Murray, London, 1973, pp. 47–8. I am grateful to Alastair Laing for pointing out to me this unindexed reference.
12 At Erddig, over which John Fowler was briefly consulted during his last illness, the brilliant white ground of the restored Chinese paper was similarly 'toned down' on John Fowler's orders. I am grateful to Merlin Waterson for discussing with me John Fowler's influence at Erddig.
13 Lees-Milne, *op. cit.* 1992, pp. 82–3
14 My thanks to Christopher Rowell for this amusing reminiscence, which does occur in the minutes for the National Trust Arts Panel meeting at Clandon.
15 Christopher Wall kindly discussed with me his and John Fowler's work at Sudbury Hall.
16 Cornforth, John, 'Clandon Park Revisited – I & II', *Country Life*, vol. cxlvi, no. 3796, 4 December 1969, pp. 1456–60, and 11 December 1969, pp. 1582–6.
17 *Country Life*, vol. cl, no. 3866, pp. 165–6.
18 Christopher Wall states that the earliest layer of colour found on the woodwork of the Staircase was indeed white, of two tones, a darker colour on the newels and a paler shade on the acanthus scrolls of the balustrade. It was a deliberate scheme, not some agent's whitewash. There was no visible trace of a grained scheme below this white layer. As found, the walls of the Staircase compartment were a pale yellowy stone colour, which Fowler intensified to a brighter yellow. He also removed brown graining from the frame of the Laguerre painting, 'gilding' it with silver leaf covered with a coat of brown varnish so as to resemble pale gold. This last was also without historical precedent.
19 *Country Life*, vol. cl, no. 3866, p. 241. Transcripts of these letters are preserved in a slim volume now entitled *Sudbury Hall – The Controversy*, in the National Trust Historic Departmental Library, which is inscribed 'For the National

Trust / The Record of a brief episode in the History of Sudbury / with best wishes / Vernon / 5 November 1978'.

20 Pamela, Countess of Onslow, 'Clandon Park: a House that was once a Home', unreferenced published article endorsed '*Vogue*, 1971, p. 65' in the Clandon Park archive of the National Trust Regional Office at Polesden Lacy. Exhaustive searches have failed to find any such article in *Vogue* for that year. My thanks to Sophie Chessum and Lucy Porten for their help in attempting to do so.

21 The scarcity of furnishings in the Trust houses John Fowler decorated may be contrasted with the abundance of chattels in the houses he decorated for private clients. At Grimsthorpe, a superfluity of furniture and decorative objects had to be carefully weeded so as to achieve the effects he wanted.

22 For Fowler's scholarship, see Cornforth, *op. cit.* 1985.

23 For John Fowler's redecoration of these houses see *Wallington Hall*, National Trust guidebook, 1994; *Montacute*, 1991; and *Lyme Park*, 1998.

24 For example, Fowler's instructions for Wallington were partly supervised by George Oakes, and partly executed by 'remote control' by Peter Orde and Sheila Pettit in the late 1960s.

25 The principal rooms of these houses. I am not suggesting that all the lesser rooms, shops, tea-rooms and common parts need retain their Fowler livery.

26 Cornforth, *op. cit.*, 1985, p. 201.

RECENT INVESTIGATIONS OF FOWLER SCHEMES

CHRISTINE SITWELL

JOHN FOWLER began his association with the National Trust in the mid-1950s when he was involved at Claydon, but it was not until 1969 that a more formal arrangement was established. It is important to recall the state of affairs within the Trust in the 1950s, when it had been given approximately fifty large houses. Several notable houses, such as Montacute and Clandon, were devoid of most their contents, and others like Knole and Stourhead had been accepted, but with insufficient funds to maintain them. Regarding the Trust's approach to interior decoration at this time, James Lees-Milne writes in his book, *People and Places*:[1]

> When it came to redecorating rooms ... [the National Trust] ... employed whatever firm

of artisans it found suitable, if it chose one at all. It is not for me to pronounce whether it held its own in this respect or failed dismally during these formative years. At all events I can claim the credit of introducing John Fowler to the Trust in the 1950s. This scholarly decorator, who with his sure sense of history, was to leave an indelible imprint upon many interiors of our grandest country houses.

John Fowler's work for the National Trust covers the period between 1956 and 1976. We are now taking the opportunity to reassess his work in a number of properties where the overall interpretation of the house is being considered. Our increased knowledge of historic interiors, the availability of archival information, and the skilled interpretation of

Figure 1 Lyme Park.
National Trust Photographic Library

Figure 2 The Entrance Hall, Lyme Park, post-Fowler. *National Trust Photographic Library*

Figure 3 (opposite) The Grand Staircase, Lyme Park, post-Fowler. *National Trust Photographic Library*

cross-sections combined with modern techniques in paint analysis, provide the necessary information to re-evaluate his original schemes. In some instances a decision has been taken, on the basis of recent evidence, to redecorate, but in others, Fowler schemes continue to sit comfortably within the overall redecoration of the house.

I would like to consider two houses where the Trust has undertaken initial investigations: Lyme Park and Clandon. Lyme Park presents the most complete project, whereas Clandon is still in the process of being re-evaluated, and the results of recent research are proving interesting.

The origins of Lyme begin in 1398, when Richard II granted the land to Piers Legh and his wife Margaret as a reward for the heroic deeds of her grandfather, Sir Thomas Danyers, at the Battle of Crécy. The present house reflects the continuing development around the remains of the Elizabethan core, the Drawing Room and Long Gallery being the principal survivors. Further additions were made in the seventeenth century but the most notable alterations were begun by Peter XII (most of Legh's male descendants

were named either Peter or Piers, hence the numerals) when, in the 1720s, he commissioned Giacomo Leoni to create the Entrance Hall, Saloon, Grand Staircase, and Bright Gallery. In the early nineteenth century Lewis Wyatt attempted to unify this piecemeal development by connecting all the staterooms on the first floor, enlarging the Dining Room, creating a Library, altering the Long Gallery and adjoining bedrooms, and redesigning the Stag Parlour. In 1903 the fashionable Edwardian decorators Philippe and Amadée Joubert made further decorative changes to the house, particularly in the Entrance Hall, Stag Parlour, Dining Room, and Library.

In 1946 the house, bereft of the core of its contents, was left to the National Trust. As it was not endowed it was leased to Stockport Corporation, who used the majority of the rooms as school facilities. Only five principal rooms were opened to the public: the Entrance Hall, Grand Staircase, Saloon, Drawing Room, and Chapel. Although furniture and paintings were lent to the house, the rooms retained a rather Spartan appearance. Faced with the problem of trying to

make the interiors presentable, the Trust sought the advice of John Fowler in the 1960s, although the redecoration programme did not begin until the 1970s.

Fowler was asked to investigate several rooms that included the Entrance Hall, Saloon, Drawing Room, and Library, as well as the two staircases, the Grand Staircase, and the smaller staircase to the Drawing Room. Many of the rooms which Fowler was to consider, particularly the Grand Staircase, retained the dark graining schemes which were probably introduced by Wyatt sometime between 1813 and 1819. The layers of discoloured varnish added to the overall feeling of Victorian gloom.

The appearance of the Entrance Hall in 1903 had been significantly altered by the Jouberts, who introduced three Mortlake tapestries and replaced the original Wyatt fireplace with a classical one based on that in the Drawing Room. At this date all the woodwork was grained and gilded and the ceiling was painted a sky colour. After investigating the room Fowler stated in his report of 1964 that:[2]

> … we found that the first colour put on was green, that there was virtually no picking-out and certainly no gilding beneath the gilding which now appears. It is possible that we detected a lighter colour which might have been a different coloured off-white, but if that was the original intention it must have almost entirely disappeared with age or with cleaning down. The only evidence of any significance in the decoration was that the pilasters of the tabernacle which are used to frame a picture, were originally fluted in trompe l'oeil in tones of the same green.

Fowler's recommendations were approved and in order to make the Entrance Hall appear lighter, the architectural elements – including the chimney piece – were painted in varying tones of stone colour, the guide for the tone of the stone being the off-whites in the Mortlake tapestries. John Cornforth, in his book *The Inspiration of the Past*, refers to Fowler's technique of using the colour of a patterned object in the room to set the tone for the paint.[3] Fowler also outlined in

great detail the tonal range of the stone colour to be used for different elements within the columns, pilasters, and entablature. For example, the reeding of the columns and pilasters was to be in the lightest off-white, the fluted shafts in the middle off-white, and the capitals and base moulds picked out in the lightest off-white. Again, according to John Cornforth:[4]

> … he conveyed the language of classicism through the varying tones … how to balance in paint the different elements of an entablature, order, wall, dado and skirting, when to bring out the flutes of a column and when to dull down detail.

In the Entrance Hall, the wall surfaces above the dado were to be painted a pale grey-green with enriched plaster mouldings picked out in a lighter tone of green. The ceiling was to be repainted white.

Fowler's scheme cannot be considered authentic. It must be remembered that the intention was to make the room feel lighter, and this new scheme would tie in with the schemes applied to the two staircases which led off the Entrance Hall.

During the recent re-evaluation of this room the removal of the nineteenth-century graining scheme by Fowler in 1972 was discussed, and it is probable that the graining may be re-instated at a future date. For the time being the scheme was considered satisfactory, particularly in light of the current presentation of the room, which includes many of the original contents.

Prior to Fowler's investigation of the Grand Staircase, the walls were cream-coloured and the stained-oak woodwork was darkened by the discoloration of the varnish. Fowler's report does not refer to paint-scrape analysis and so it is assumed that his recommendations were based on his overall brief to lighten the appearance of the rooms. He recommended that all the discoloured varnish should be stripped from the dado, newels, balusters, columns, and their entablature, and that the remaining varnished brown joinery should be painted a stone colour. The wall surfaces were to be

Figure 4 The Saloon, Lyme Park, post-Fowler. *National Trust Photographic Library*

painted a buff apricot using the existing cream-coloured scheme as the undercoat and the window reveals were to be painted a stone off-white colour, while the recently painted ceiling only required cleaning and re-gilding.

The stripped woodwork has, with time, developed a bleached and parched appearance. The desire to improve its appearance provided an incentive to examine the wall colour of the staircase and reconsider the decorative schemes of the Bright Gallery and the smaller Drawing Room Staircase, which lead off the Grand Staircase at the first floor level. Examination of the two inventories of 1879 and 1929 also prompted a reappraisal of the picture-hang on the staircase.

The combination of paint scrapes and paint analysis revealed a paint stratigraphy of at least eleven decorative schemes. The earliest decoration was a grey-white distemper, followed by two green-based schemes, an apricot scheme, a pink scheme, two deep-red-based schemes, followed by three schemes of varying cream tonality and finally the pink Fowler scheme applied in the 1970s. Archival information as well as the existence of painted areas covered by later fixtures helped to create a tentative dating system for the paint layers. Comparative research in the Bright Gallery suggested that the two deep-red schemes were applied during the late nineteenth and early twentieth centuries.

It was decided that these areas, as well as the Saloon, were to be presented as they appeared when the house was decorated by the Jouberts at the turn of the century. The walls were painted a bright red, the bleached woodwork was darkened and the joinery was re-grained. It should be noted that during the initial discussions of redecoration options, the retention of Fowler's pink wall scheme had been considered and the primary focus was the woodwork. However, as the approach for the representation of the whole house began to develop, his scheme no

longer fitted into the original robust Edwardian decorations created by the Jouberts.

In the Saloon the nineteenth-century installation of the Grinling Gibbons carvings, salvaged from the New Parlour demolished by Wyatt when creating the current Dining Room, created a significant design element in the room. In his report Fowler describes the carvings as having 'an unattractive stain'. He recommended that the oak panels and the carving be stripped in order to give the Palladian proportions of this room a greater degree of light and shade, and also suggested that the white and gold plasterwork ceiling should be cleaned and touched up if considered necessary. Fowler's recommendations for the lightening of the panelling and carvings were considered a success at the time. The initial honey-coloured appearance helped to reduce the amount of dark graining that was so prevalent throughout the house. Unfortunately, the use of bleach and caustic soda to remove the stain eventually created the blotchy and dry appearance which was certainly visible by the mid-1990s. The limewood carvings were now darker than the panelling.

The Trust's decision to darken the panelling and slightly lighten the carvings reflects the overall approach of reinstating the earlier Joubert scheme of 1907.

It is in the Drawing Room that Fowler made the most extensive recommendations and, in a sense, allowed his personal preferences to come into play. He refers to the room as: '... a curiously dingy room in need of a great deal of pulling together'. His intention was to 'humanize' it by adding an old-fashioned Turkish carpet to go in front of the fireplace and several Victorian country-house armchairs and a sofa. John Cornforth records that:[5]

> In his early days, Fowler evidently had little interest in providing comfort, but it became an essential ingredient of his mature work. His generous chairs and sofas of unfussy shape and looking as if they hailed from a smoking room or a library, not only look but are comfortable.

He also suggested removing the two late-eighteenth-century English gilt-wood side-tables and replacing them with a pair of gilt rococo console tables, similar to the ones in the Wyatt dining room. According to Cornforth, Fowler liked to add 'a dash of French' in a room.[6]

With regard to the colour scheme, he suggested that the reveals of all the windows and the sashes, where possible, should be

Figure 6 (left) The Saloon, Clandon, post-Fowler. *National Trust Photographic Library*

Figure 7 (right) Cross section (×100) of a sample removed from the dado of the Saloon, Clandon. The section shows the original dark green at the lowest level (wooden substrate detached) and the intermediate blue scheme which Fowler's paint scrape analysis identified as being the original scheme. Fowler's blue scheme can be seen at the top of the section.

painted a stone off-white as this would lighten the room. The ceiling was to be painted in two tones of bone-coloured off-white with some alteration to the gilding of the ceiling. The plaster part of the chimney piece was to be painted in a similar fashion, with the lower stonework stripped of its paint. Various suggestions were made for the frieze, ranging from a stone colour to a soft red to repainting, or even retaining, the existing plum colour. His final recommendation was that all the oak should be stripped – which again indicated his overall intention, which was to lighten the room.

That the suggested colour schemes for the room were not based on historical precedence is indicated by the various options for the colour of the frieze. Fowler's recommendations were a mixture of his personal taste and his intention of fulfilling the Trust's desire to reduce the gloomy Victorian feel of the house. The Trust did not undertake any of Fowler's suggestions, partly due to its uncertainty about his recommendations and to financial constraints. But this may be seen as a fortunate decision as the room is also now considered to be an important interior decoration by Wyatt, and the 'dingy appearance' referred to by Fowler was enormously improved by careful cleaning. Much of the original furniture for the room has been returned to the house through donations from the family and purchases at auctions.

Fowler's work at Lyme must be viewed in its proper context. In those early years only a handful of rooms were open to the public and the Trust was not in a position to formulate a long-term plan for the house, let alone a defined approach to the decorative schemes. The Trust's intention was to lighten the overall appearance and to create a harmonious interior using the limited contents.

Although Fowler undertook paint scrapes in the Entrance Hall, they were not extensive and do not appear to have had significant bearing on his final recommendations. His approach, however, suited the time and requirements of the Trust. During the 1990s the Trust has had the opportunity to re-evaluate his schemes in light of a more considered approach to the overall appearance of the interiors. Many more rooms, particularly the family rooms, as well as the Library, Dining Room, and Stag Library, are now on view and investigations of these rooms have revealed that there has been an extensive overlaying of schemes during the centuries. However, the Trust has decided that the most significant period for the presentation of the house is that of the late nineteenth century. Many of the former contents of these rooms have now been returned to the house and are an integral part of this decorative scheme. It has been a long evolution but Lyme Park is now assuming it own identity, exhibiting important decorative schemes from the late nineteenth and early twentieth centuries.

Clandon Park has been the home of the Onslow family since 1641. The original Elizabethan house was redesigned circa 1731 by Giacomo Leoni. The house was given to the National Trust in 1956 and, like Lyme Park, was devoid of most of its core contents, these having been sold over a number of years beginning with the great sale of 1781. Fortunately, a generous benefactor, Mrs David Gubbay, bequeathed her fine collection of eighteenth-century furniture, textiles, and porcelain, together with the residue of her estate, to the Trust in 1968. Although the taxman took a sizeable chunk of the residue, further financial assistance was received from Mr and Mrs Kenneth Levy. These generous gifts enabled the Trust to improve the dilapidated condition

believed to be the original eighteenth-century decoration. Removing layers of distemper from the ceiling, he revealed an elaborate colour scheme of blue and cream. He also discovered blue, red, and cream on the cornice and evidence of a blue scheme on the walls. Recent paint analysis has revealed that the Saloon was originally panelled from floor to cornice and had been decorated in a dark green (lead white tinted with Prussian blue, ochre, and charcoal black) applied over a dark grey undercoat (lead white tinted with charcoal black).[8] It is probable that Fowler's paint scrapes removed the upper paint layers and revealed an intermediate blue decoration – which led him to believe that the original scheme was blue.

It has now been established that the ceiling and cornice were originally decorated in a white distemper while the panelling was painted in a deep green. Archival research has revealed that the Saloon was repainted in 1879 by the fourth Earl who, to compensate for years of neglect, was undertaking major refurbishment at this period. Most of the original distemper decoration would have been washed off in preparation for the application of the later scheme and was therefore missed by Fowler, who then assumed that he had found the eighteenth-century scheme. Fowler's treatment of the overmantle of the chimney piece, a dramatic combination of black and white, may be based on his discovery of an earlier scheme of 1879, when it was painted in white distemper and a dark brown.[9]

Fowler's final scheme was a mixture of colours discovered through paint scrapes but adjusted by his personal taste. The polished mahogany doors were painted white, which one assumes was more satisfactory in the context of the final scheme. With regard to the furnishings, Fowler removed most of the existing furniture, which gave the room a drawing-room feel in order to complement the austerity of the Marble Hall.

It also placed greater emphasis on the plasterwork and its new colour scheme. Fowler's approach to the ceiling does highlight his concern with preserving original

of the house and to implement a programme of interior redecoration. John Fowler was invited to advise on the redecoration, focusing on the eighteenth-century origins and the arrangement of the principal rooms to include the recently acquired gift from Mrs Gubbay and the remains of the indigenous Onslow collection.

His work at Clandon between 1968 and 1971 was perhaps the turning point in the Trust's approach to interior decoration, in that Fowler attempted to establish the previous historical decorative schemes by using paint scrapes more extensively to supplement his own understanding of eighteenth-century decoration. He was given a broader palette than at Lyme to create his final schemes. It is worth mentioning that Fowler lived close to Clandon and therefore was able to spend a considerable amount of time there – as John Cornforth records, 'he grew to love what many people find a distinctly unlovable house'.[7]

In the Saloon, Fowler undertook paint-scrape analysis which revealed what he

Figure 9 The Saloon, Clandon before redecoration showing test scrapes carried out by Fowler. *National Trust Photographic Library*

schemes where possible as opposed to the wholesale repainting of this feature. Although this is a sensibility reflected in much of the work carried out by the Trust today, it was certainly considered innovative at the time.

In the Marble Hall Fowler was in his element, as he viewed classical architecture as subtle variations of colour. John Cornforth's own appraisal of this room reconfirms this approach:[10]

> His painting of the hall still seems a triumph of architectural painting, of subtle variations in the tones and textures of white that not only gives added life to the whole concept and ornamentation but makes up for the deliberate austerity of the furnishings.

His paint scrapes in this room were misleading as once again the marbling he uncovered was not the original eighteenth-century scheme but the 1879 decoration. However, he retained this scheme, carefully cleaning off the distemper from the lower order of the columns and then extending the marbling on to the base blocks and the skirting.

As Tim Knox (p. 16) and Peter Inskip (pp. 6–7) mention, Fowler's interpretation of

the Green Drawing Room involved the removal of the existing brocatelle to reveal the underlying flock wallpaper, which he then modified. Recent paint analysis has established that the scheme Fowler applied to the ceiling is purely decorative and has no historical basis. However, Fowler often used the colours of patterns found within the room as the basis for new decorative schemes. Christopher Wall, who was Historic Buildings Representative for the Trust and worked with Fowler on several occasions, refers to the fact that:[11]

> … he invariably chose patterns before colour, establishing in his mind the needs of progression first, then those of scale and only afterwards the medium and the colour.

The detailed paint research and analysis being carried out at Clandon seeks to supplement the existing documentary evidence and provide a clearer understanding of the decorative history of the house. It has already highlighted the flaws in Fowler's approach in that he misinterpreted his paint scrapes where he used them as a basis for the redecoration. It also reveals the extent to which he used his own interpretative skills

Figure 10 The Marble Hall, Clandon, post-Fowler. *National Trust Photographic Library*

when trying to bring balance to a room's interior. However, to his credit and bearing in mind that his work predates the availability of modern methods of paint analysis, he treated the evidence from scrapes of past work with great regard. Cornforth notes: 'he strove for beauty within the limits of that evidence rather than a strict reproduction'.[12] It is easy to criticize his work with the advantage of hindsight and our current attitudes to the interpretation of historic interiors. It is the dichotomy between Fowler's understanding of historic interiors and his contemporary practices which has created problematic interiors that now require careful consideration; but as Christopher Rowell writes in the new guidebook for Clandon: 'Fowler's work is in itself a landmark in the history of late twentieth-century country house decoration'.[13]

Acknowledgement

I would like to thank my colleagues, James Rothwell (Lyme Park) and Christopher Rowell (Clandon), for their generous assistance in the preparation of this paper.

References

1 Lees-Milne, James, *People and Places: Country House Donors and the National Trust*, Murray, London, 1992, p. 17.
2 John Fowler unpublished report, held by the National Trust.
3 Cornforth, John, *The Inspiration of the Past: Country House Taste in the Twentieth Century*, Viking, London, 1985, p. 161.
4 Ibid., p. 162.
5 Ibid., p. 163.
6 Ibid.
7 Ibid., p. 218.
8 Hassall, Catherine, 'Paint Analysis at Clandon Park', unpublished report, June 2001.
9 Ibid.
10 Cornforth, *op. cit.*, p. 217.
11 Ibid., p. 162.
12 Ibid., p. 231.
13 *Clandon Park*, National Trust guidebook, 2001

INSPIRED BY THE PAST?

PATRICK BATY

THREE YEARS before he died, John Fowler collaborated with the architectural historian, John Cornforth, on a book entitled *English Decoration in the 18th Century*.[1] With a complete chapter devoted to the subject, it was, until I discovered the works of Dr Ian Bristow, the first important source of information on the historical use of paint and colour that I had found. The references and bibliography alone provided me with many months of useful foraging.

Their introduction suggested that much of John Fowler's approach to the decoration of country houses, and consequently that of a later generation of interior decorators, could be found within the ensuing pages. The second edition of their work appeared in 1986, some nine years after John Fowler had died. Quite unforgivably, I had let my copy lie unopened for nearly fifteen years, and it was only in preparation for a talk given at an earlier conference that I came to reread and review its contents.

The aim of this paper is to provide an overview of their chapter on paint and colour, and to see how relevant it is nowadays as a secondary source for those working on the restoration of painted decoration in historic buildings. Reference has also been made to a later work of John Cornforth's, *The Inspiration of the Past*,[2] which examines Fowler's contribution to the English interior.

I never met John Fowler, but have talked briefly with John Cornforth about how their book was written. If I have understood the facts correctly, Mr Fowler provided much of the inspiration and, over the course of many conversations and at a time when he was already a very sick man, explained his approach to historical decoration. His co-author kept the project focused, he listened, looked for the evidence,[3] provided an enormous number of his own references, and put pen to paper, bringing out the first edition of their book in 1974.

This book introduced me to many primary sources in the field of paint research, and to those in related fields. The treatment of floors, upholstery, lighting, heating, and picture hanging was dealt with in depth, and it soon became a vital source of reference in a world poorly served with such detail. Indeed, one of its main purposes was to serve as a basic guide on the history of decoration for the National Trust's Historic Buildings Representatives.[4]

On rereading the chapter concerning paint and colour one can form a clearer idea of the individual contribution made by each author. However, it is perhaps this attempt to blend the theoretical with the practical that now causes a certain unease.

It should be stressed that much has happened since their joint work first appeared and, largely because of Ian Bristow's magnificent contribution to the field, our understanding is now greater.[5] What follows must not, therefore, be seen as criticism, merely as an illustration of how the practices and views expressed by one of the most significant interior decorators of the twentieth century must be regarded as just those, and not necessarily as an accurate exposition of earlier procedures.

When the book was first written a number of the techniques now available to examine the sequence of paints applied to a surface were in their infancy. In spite of referring to them, the authors seemed slow in recognizing their potential, and often fell into the same trap that they warned against, that of believing that something was old, or even original, merely because it looked it. Increasingly it is understood that it is necessary to examine both the physical and documentary evidence before coming to any conclusions. Until recent architectural paint research was carried out at Newhailes, in East Lothian, for example, it was thought that the Dining Room displayed its original scheme of the 1740s.[6] This is now known not to be the case.[7]

The Balcony Room at Dyrham Park, in Gloucestershire, and the Boudoir at Attingham Park, in Shropshire, were both described by Fowler and Cornforth as displaying 'untouched' or 'original' paint. However, some years before the second edition appeared, it was revealed that both displayed later overpainting.[8]

Ironically, Fowler's repainting of the Saloon at Clandon Park, which formed the basis of a number of their assertions, has now been shown to have been incorrectly interpreted.[9] (Inskip p. 5, Knox p. 16, Sitwell p. 28) The work was carried out following the making of paint scrapes, the futility of which will be discussed later in this paper.

It was this work at Clandon that provided the authors with the precedent for using different tones of colour on early-eighteenth-century plasterwork.[10] However, we now know that the scheme that was 'restored' by John Fowler was the one applied in c.1879, not the original 1735 one.

Tellingly, they admitted that no eighteenth-century instructions had been discovered for painting a room in the way that they described in their section entitled *The Problems of Painting Architectural Decoration*.[11] This description best summarizes the style that we now associate with John Fowler, a style that is still being reproduced in both private houses and houses open to the public. Typically it involves the use of such devices as an off-black on the skirting fascia, the picking out of mouldings, and the application of three tints of off-white on panelled doors.

The authors acknowledged that the only reference to the use of three tones of colour is among the Osterley papers. If they were referring to the David Adamson bill for painting at Osterley in the 1770s,[12] they have overstated the case. Certainly, the ceiling of the Drawing Room was picked in with 'superfine green, pink, dark purple and sky blue colour', and the doors to Mr Child's Dressing Room were green with white mouldings, but nothing suggesting three tones of the same colour has been encountered.

They mentioned the Adamson bill earlier in the chapter, expressing surprise at the extensive use of oil paint, and claiming that there was a 'definite attempt to create contrasts between flat and shiny paint'.[13] Evidence provided by similar accounts of the period[14] suggests that oil paint was the conventional treatment for the fine rooms of such a house. To suggest that there was 'a definite attempt' to create such contrasts might, again, be an over-statement.

Likening decoration to cookery, the authors of *English Decoration in the 18th Century* told us that:[15]

> Memorable cookery is based on flair and freedom of interpretation, and so is the best decoration: slavish adherence to the pattern books seldom produced the most successful results.

It is perhaps this tendency to fall back on the unmeasurables of taste and opinion, rather than precedent, which caused me most difficulty when first considering Fowler's approach to historical decoration. How does one know when one is looking at good 'cookery', or at a scheme that reflects precedent? Who decides when the 'original magic and balance' of a room has been restored, for example, and how is the evidence presented?

At this stage, perhaps, we should ask ourselves about the sort of decorative treatment given to historic buildings. Should that accorded to a house open to the public, or owned by a national heritage organization, differ from that in a house in private ownership? To simplify matters, this paper will concern itself solely with the former.

It is in the last paragraph of their book, in talking about Sudbury Hall, Derbyshire, that the authors explained that the aim of the restoration of a sparsely furnished house, whose sole use was to be shown to visitors, was to give the visitors 'an experience that is as rich and enjoyable as possible'.[16] Attitudes to the display of such houses have changed since the 1970s, and many now appreciate that something can be learned by showing a house 'warts and all', while still aiming for a rich and enjoyable experience. Whenever 'restoration', of the type now recognized by the Burra Charter,[17] was mentioned, one sensed that it did not meet with their approval. Words such as 'academic', 'frozen', or 'pedantry' were used, and care urged to avoid the 'slavish renewal of the misguided taste of the day before yesterday'.[18]

On the one hand, theirs is a serious book containing a wealth of sources on every aspect of interior decoration, with references to numerous letters, journals, bills, images, and early published works. On the other, they appear to have been highly selective in the interpretation of these references.

In *English Decoration in the 18th Century*, Messrs Fowler and Cornforth provided a very comprehensive list of books concerned with house painting, colour, and fine art, the implication being that they studied all these works prior to writing their chapter on paint and colour. However, having suggested that correlation with these manuals would be of considerable assistance to those trying to identify colours from accounts and inventories, and that such an exercise would enable colours to be produced for restorations, the authors then betrayed a consistent lack of understanding of the technical details in those selfsame texts.

Many of the instances cited below will no doubt be regarded as petty, and it is certainly

true that knowledge of early practices has advanced significantly only in recent years.[19] However, when one rereads the chapter with the benefit of current information, the large number of misunderstandings leaves one with a strong feeling that Fowler's work owed less to historical precedent, than to received notions of the past.

For instance, the authors told us that according to Robert Dossie's *The Handmaid to the Arts* eggshell paint was actually derived from eggshells. The reference was in fact to a little-used watercolour pigment,[20] not, as might be assumed, to the mid-sheen finish used in twentieth-century decoration.

They continued to display their lack of understanding of the technical aspects of historical precedent by pointing out that Dossie did not mention 'dead white' among his list of white pigments. But this is hardly surprising because 'dead white' was a flat white finish – a painting process – not a pigment.

More importantly, Fowler and Cornforth referred to a description of how to paint a room 'three times in oil' in William Butcher's rare house-painting manual of 1821.[21] They described it as being a very similar process to the one that they then outlined at length, and which they told the reader was 'based on a combination of personal experience and historical precedent'.[22]

I own a copy of the 1821 work and, having made a comparison of the two descriptions, can see no reason why they have cited it as a source.

By juxtaposing a synopsis of Fowler and Cornforth's recommended approach to painting a room with the traditional method outlined by William Butcher,[23] and by providing a brief commentary, my concerns should become clear:

Butcher: For the first coat – take the best white lead, mix it well with two-thirds of linseed oil, and one-third of turpentine; add driers, then lay it on as a thin and even coat. Once dry, this coat should be rubbed down, and any holes filled.

Fowler and Cornforth: The surface should be primed with a white-lead primer, the holes and cracks should then be filled. The surface is then rubbed down, using progressively finer grades of glass paper. A coat of transparent shellac polish is then applied.

The composition of the first coat is basically similar.[24] Nowadays, one winces to see the modern authors unknowingly suggest the hazardous practice of the dry rubbing down of a lead-painted surface, thus releasing a cloud of toxic particles into the air.[25] The light use of a wet pumice stone, or wet and dry paper, might have been mentioned if they were describing the correct method of wet rubbing down. Having used one or two different grades of sandpaper, and (presumably) removed much of the first coat, they then applied shellac, rather than a second coat of primer.

Their next process was slightly more elaborate than that described in the original text:

Butcher: The second coat was to be mixed as before, although fewer driers were to be added.

Fowler and Cornforth: Two coats of undercoat were next applied. We were told that as white eggshell (a modern alkyd resin titanium based paint) tended to discolour and darken when used by itself, it was better to use a mixture of 50 per cent white eggshell and 50 per cent flat white undercoat as the last undercoat before the final colour was applied.

The final process was somewhat different to the original:

Butcher: The third coat was mixed using half oil and half turpentine. A colourless drier in the form of white copperas (zinc sulphate) and a small quantity of blue or black pigment were added to reduce the inherent yellowness of the white.

Fowler and Cornforth: The final coat should have stainers added and be given a flat finish. The alkyd resin eggshell paint could be thinned with pure turpentine, and sometimes a very small quantity of linseed oil could be added. This, we were told, would allow the paint to 'flow' more easily if it seemed 'ropy' (i.e. thick and streaky).

In the next paragraph, however, Fowler and Cornforth went on to quote the late Morgan Philips, who said:[26]

Most of us now understand that old paint has not only colour but a ropy textured appearance, usually showing pronounced brush marks.

Quite why this quote was included is unclear, especially as we had just been told to add linseed oil in order to prevent a 'ropy' appearance, and to avoid a 'dead mechanical finish'. Surely this latter, itself, is a further contradiction, as a smoother finish would be more 'dead' and 'mechanical' than a 'ropy' one?

From a technical point of view, one might question the wisdom of mixing turpentine and linseed oil with a ready-formulated product that contained neither, and which had been carefully produced in order to flow, and to cover well.

The authors then stated that oil would tend to give a glossy appearance, and so should be used very sparingly. However, the addition of linseed oil would not only make it glossier, it would also increase the chance of the paint yellowing. This was, presumably, why they had suggested mixing the white eggshell with flat undercoat to produce a whiter base coat. Would it not have been better to have left the paint alone?

It might seem unduly pedantic to criticize their technique, but it appears to be more appropriate for the painting of furniture rather than architectural surfaces. The citing of William Butcher's method of 1821 is completely spurious, and their process appears to have no basis in recognizable historical precedent.

No doubt, such a long-winded process would add to the cost of the work. Indeed, the authors admitted that their process might sound a very long-drawn-out and costly one, but they claimed that it was the only way to avoid a dead mechanical finish that is 'so unpleasing in a large room in an old house'.[27] However, the unnecessary complexity of the process, cloaked as it was in mock-historical garb, seems to have been highly prized by Fowler's clients.

To give a greater sense of depth and texture to the colour, the authors told us that the final coat of paint might be applied in different ways, the most usual of which were brush graining, stippling, glaze painting, and dragging. All of these fashionable finishes, like the actual method of painting which had just been described, 'are based on historical precedents'.[28] Once again, an element of distortion had crept into their text, unless of course a more recent origin was implied by their use of the word 'historical'.

Certainly, Dossie mentioned 'glazing',[29] but in the context of fine art and small painted objects, not the decoration of walls or woodwork. Similarly, when he referred to colours that are transparent in water, rather than oil, he called these 'washing' colours – a term familiar to watercolourists. David Ramsay Hay, in the sixth edition of his *Laws of Harmonious Colouring* of 1847, was one of the first authors to mention a stippling brush, but this was for laying off a flatting coat on painted walls, and certainly not a coloured glaze.[30] Brush graining, stippling, and dragging were actually processes used in the early years of the twentieth century, but could this legitimately be considered 'historical' when Fowler and Cornforth's work was published in 1974, only fifty or so years later?[31]

As if to acknowledge some of the doubts that might have been raised by more knowledgeable readers, Fowler and Cornforth admitted that glazing:[32]

... is a method that is very difficult to analyse through scrapes, because the glazes are so thin that they hardly ever survive and also because they are effected by the action of the oils in the paint.

Once again, we were being asked to believe that in spite of the lack of physical evidence, their reading of historical sources had provided them with this information.

Furthermore, they said:[33]

To anyone concerned with restoration who encounters these techniques used in historic interiors today, the questions that immediately spring to mind are firstly 'are the results authentic' and 'are the methods authentic'. The answer to both cannot be an unequivocal 'yes' for the mediums are not exactly the same as those used in the past, and consequently results have to be achieved in a different way. Nor indeed have the methods been conceived for restorations: they have been worked out for the decoration of private houses before there was a demand for the kind of 'academic restorations' that is now developing in England.

However, they assured us that:[34]

... they do correspond to the methods described in the books mentioned at the beginning of the chapter.

In writing of John Fowler's contribution to the English interior in his book *The Inspiration of the Past*, John Cornforth illustrated a number of colour samples. These were produced by Fowler in 1947 for Christopher Hussey, who was preparing a pamphlet on external colour for the Georgian Group.[35] Annotations on the reverse of each suggest that they were made up from combinations of the following pigments: white, black, yellow ochre, raw umber, Venetian red, burnt Sienna, crimson lake, vermilion, emerald green, chrome yellow, and cobalt blue.

Keen students of the architectural use of paint and colour in the eighteenth century will see that only one of the eight combinations of colour would have been possible at that time. A number of the pigments, such as emerald green, cobalt blue, and chrome yellow, were not invented until the following century; others, such as crimson lake, were too fugitive to use externally; while vermilion and burnt sienna were expensive, and therefore inappropriate, for large-scale use.

Once again, these choices appear to have been based on whimsy and taste alone, certainly not on historical precedent.

Mr Cornforth tells us that John Fowler began to use strong colours in the 1950s, in particular the Italian pinks and orange–terracotta colours that he liked in halls and staircases,[36] the most striking of these perhaps being the Wyatt Cloisters in Wilton House, Wiltshire, with an apricot terracotta stippled over a yellow ground, and the vestibule and staircase of the library at Christ Church, Oxford.

The liking of pink may have come from the American decorator Nancy Lancaster's use of it in the Entrance Hall of her house, Kelmarsh Hall in Northamptonshire.[37] (Sühr, p. 55, Figure 6) We are told in an earlier passage that seven coats of distemper were used to reproduce the pink which was originally seen in the Hall at Lady Islington's house, Rushbrooke Hall, in Suffolk.[38]

Cross-section examination[39] of a number of paint samples from the walls at Kelmarsh revealed no evidence of seven coats having been applied.[40] This is just as well, as to apply that many coats of an oil-bound distemper[41] would have been technically naive. There is a tendency for this sort of paint to delaminate, or peel away from the wall, once a certain number of coats have been applied.[42] One presumes that the painter used his common sense and own initiative when given the specification by Mr Fowler.

The pinks may also have come from the chalky grounds of the eighteenth- and nineteenth-century Chinese wallpapers that Fowler studied when he was training as a painter of wallpaper in Thornton Smith's studio in the 1920s. Probably the most important influence was his sight of the villas of the Veneto during a Georgian Group tour in the mid-1950s.[43]

His painter's eye and his historical sense, we were told, made him prefer oil-bound water paint to modern emulsion paint,[44] which he 'despised'. It was the dry look of water paint that he liked and thought more important than a perfect finish or long life; 'also it gave the worn effect of old colour if applied in thin glazes'.[45] Although acknowledged as being inauthentic, Mr Cornforth told us that it did however reproduce, in modern materials, the textured effects which could not be avoided

in previous generations, because of the poor grinding of pigment.

Incidentally, the authors appear not to have fully understood the nature of soft distemper, which they described as being made from 'ball whiting broken down over heat with size and water'. The traditional method of making it involves the soaking of whiting (chalk) in cold water followed by the addition of a warm glue size. This was allowed to cool to a jelly-like consistency before being applied.[46]

They described soft distemper as giving a dry fresco-like effect that appeals today but did not appeal to eighteenth-century taste:[47]

> … for according to a mid 18th century dictionary in the Victoria and Albert Museum 'The greatest disadvantage of distemper is, that it has no glittering, and all its colours look dead.'

In spite of having just told us of the interchangeable meaning, in the context of paint, of the words 'dead' and 'flat', they seemed to have forgotten this other meaning. Could this reference suggest the unthinkable – that a flat finish was not always desirable in the first half of the eighteenth century? What could John Smith – another of their sources – have meant when he wrote:[48]

> Take Notice, That all simple Colours used in House Painting, appear much more beautiful and lustrous, when they appear as if glazed over with a Varnish …

Chester Jones, in his book on Colefax & Fowler,[49] tells us that to this day the company often apply paint using techniques that were first 'brought back into favour' by John Fowler, and then developed by him and George Oakes to evoke the softness of old tired paintwork.[50] The same author tells us that the paint is put on thinly as glazes over either ground colour or white. It is then given a coat of flat varnish to protect the vulnerable surface, as well as to leave that 'dry' finish which is 'essential to the look of old paintwork'.[51]

As mentioned already, this form of painting has more to do with the painting of furniture than that of architectural elements.

Historical precedent is not what this technique is based on, yet it is this approach which, until the so-called 'academic' restorations of recent years, guided our hand in the painting of historical interiors.

Such was Fowler's influence that it appears that his reported words to Ian McCallum, 'Now, child, a colour can go muddy if you do not show the undercoat through',[52] are still heeded. Even now there is a belief, in some quarters, that lead paint was transparent. This is indeed odd because, for over three hundred years, and in spite of its known toxicity, it was used for its opacity.[53] Similarly we were told that distemper gives a subtly 'irregular effect', and so techniques resembling the paint effects so popular in the early 1980s are still being applied on the walls of period rooms in museums and country houses open to the public.[54]

There are many useful quotes in *English Decoration in the 18th Century*, and it is perhaps ironic that the unfortunate effects displayed in these recently decorated rooms might have been avoided had one of them been made more of by the authors. They provided a description of the painting of a room taken from a letter of 1767. This related to the application of three coats of distemper, and tellingly concluded by saying that: 'This method succeeded so well that it is all one colour, and looks extremely well …'.[55] Might this be taken to mean that a solid colour was desirable?

Attention has been drawn to one of the many eccentric treatments that Fowler gave to a historic interior in the example of the Saloon at Wallington, in Northumberland. Having carried out paint scrapes, and come to the conclusion that originally, in the 1740s, the walls were lilac and the plasterwork white, John Fowler reversed this, painting the walls white and the plasterwork lilac. If such reversals were considered justified, one wonders why it was even felt necessary to take scrapes. As a one-off example this may not have been such a problem, but were the visiting public told what had happened here, or were they allowed to assume that this was an earlier, 'restored', scheme?

Another example, perhaps better known, is West Wycombe Park in Buckinghamshire, transformed in the 1740s from a Queen Anne house into a broadly Palladian one. Here, as the late Sir Francis Dashwood tells us in his history of the house,[56] he employed John Fowler to help restore the house after the War. The walls of the Saloon were, he says, painted a 'startling yellow' and then glazed, in a manner similar to that at Nancy Lancaster's drawing room at the back of her shop in 39 Brook Street, London.[57] Mrs Lancaster advised the Dashwoods to retain the nineteenth-century graining on the dado, as she considered white 'so boring'.[58]

In the Music Room, Fowler stripped off the nineteenth-century pink wallpaper and was lucky to find traces of what he believed to be the original red ochre. After applying an undercoat of white, he and Hal Baxby spent three days 'using the sponging technique' that they had learnt as apprentices together.[59]

Once again, no mention is made in the guidebook and it would appear that the colours and processes used by Fowler at houses such as Wallington and West Wycombe bore more relation to the twentieth century than to the eighteenth. No doubt many visitors will have associated these schemes with the furniture and paintings, and come away with distorted notions of historical design. In houses such as this, which are open to the public, confused messages are so often being given. Small wonder that, having been softened up by such sights, the public is confused as to which genuinely constitute historical paint colours.

Both Chester Jones and John Cornforth tell us of the benefits of 'scrapes', and we learn that John Fowler would use them to discover the nature of past colour schemes. Indeed, one still reads of colours being matched to paint scrapes.[60] One wonders if such credence would be placed on this sort of process if the practitioners understood the distortions that can take place.

The problem of relying on scrapes can be seen in an area of scraped paint in the Empress Josephine's Music Room at Malmaison, near

Paris, in France. A photograph taken in 1996 shows the results of the 1983 redecoration based on scrapes. During that thirteen-year period, the scraped area of the capital has become much less dark as a result of exposure to ultraviolet light in the form of daylight. The green paint that was matched to the (then) freshly exposed scrape now acts as a permanent reminder of the folly of ill-considered scraping.

Serving as a further example are the paint colours found in a sixty-year-old paint sample book, on one side as they were when the book was first opened, and on the other after lengthy exposure to UV light. One can imagine how different a decorative scheme would be based on the two sets of colours!

Towards the end of the chapter entitled 'Colour and the painter's craft' in Fowler and Cornforth's *English Decoration in the 18th Century* we are told that: '… it would be dangerous to divide the 18th century into two distinct periods …'.[61] Surely they were not suggesting that a Palladian interior of the first quarter of the eighteenth century might be treated in the same way as an Adam interior of the last quarter?

Now, before I am accused of an unwarranted assault on two authors who are not in a position to answer back, I must emphasize that my purpose in questioning their approach is purely a concern with the treatment of historic interiors in buildings open to the public.

A gifted and innovative decorator John Fowler might have been, but to suggest that his treatment of historic interiors is worth anything more than a large chapter in the history of interior design would be asking too much. Due consideration should be given to the work carried out by him. Let us ensure, however, that it is as a significant twentieth-century decorator that he is remembered, and not as one working with historical precedent or scholarly research guiding his hand.

In summary, the materials and methods used by John Fowler were altogether closer to those that we employ today. As far as preserving examples of his work is concerned,

this might be done on a house-by-house basis. Some of the better examples might be kept, while those produced on an 'off day' might be replaced by schemes that have more relevance to the facts known about the house.

In spite of the foregoing, *English Decoration in the 18th Century* is a highly significant work and should be studied, albeit with the care taken when studying any work that blends opinion with fact. As the authors themselves said of the study of historic decoration:[62]

> … if the aim is to try to develop an objective approach to decoration and restoration, it is necessary to try to understand how and why we look at the past in the way we do and to be aware of what influences there have been on country houses in the course of this century.

No one can deny the enormous influence of John Fowler, and it is only by now questioning his own approach that we can possibly hope for greater objectivity in our treatment of historic buildings.

References

1 Fowler, John and Cornforth, John, *English Decoration in the 18th Century*, 2nd edition, Barrie & Jenkins, London, 1986.

2 Cornforth, John, *The Inspiration of the Past: Country House Taste in the Twentieth Century*, Viking, London, 1985.

3 Cornforth, John, 'John Fowler and the National Trust', in *National Trust Studies*, National Trust, London, 1979, pp. 39–49.

4 Cornforth, *op. cit.* 1985, p. 221.

5 Bristow, Ian C., *Architectural Colour in British Interiors 1615–1840* and *Interior House-Painting Colours and Technology 1615–1840*, both published by Yale University Press, London, 1996.

6 Cornforth, John, 'Newhailes, East Lothian', in *Country Life*, 21 November 1996, vol. cxc no. 47 pp. 46–51 and 28 November 1996, vol. cxc no. 48 pp. 42–7.

7 Baty, Patrick, *Newhailes House, East Lothian: A Report on the Decorative Schemes Following an Examination of the Painted Surfaces in Various Areas*, prepared for the National Trust for Scotland, 26 November 1998.

8 Bristow, Ian C., 'Repainting Eighteenth-Century Interiors', in *ASCHB Transactions*, vol. 6, 1981, pp. 25–33. See also Bristow, Ian C., 'The Balcony

Room at Dyrham', in *National Trust Studies*, National Trust, London, 1980, pp. 140–6. John Cornforth explained in his 'Note to the Second Edition' that he had only made changes of a technical, editorial nature, in order not to lose the voice of his co-author.

9 Sitwell, Christine, 'Recent Investigations of Fowler Schemes', this volume, pp. 21–30.

10 Fowler and Cornforth, *op. cit.* 1986, p. 262.

11 Ibid., pp. 180–3.

12 *Painters work done for Robert Child Esq. at Osterley in the years '72, '73 and 1774. By David Adamson.* A transcript is in the Department of Furniture and Woodwork of the Victoria & Albert Museum.

13 Fowler and Cornforth, *op. cit.* 1986, p. 179.

14 An example being John Tasker's detailed bill for painting at 20 Portman Square, London (Home House), which survives in the Cambridge Record Office. The work was carried out in 1796. I am grateful to Dr John Martin Robinson for this information.

15 Fowler and Cornforth, *op. cit.* 1986, p. 174.

16 Ibid., p. 266.

17 Australia ICOMOS *Charter for the Conservation of Places of Cultural Significance* (known as the 'Burra Charter'), Australia ICOMOS, 1981. Article 9 states that the aim of restoration '... is to preserve and reveal the aesthetic and historic value of the monument and is based on respect for original material and authentic documents'.

18 Fowler and Cornforth, *op. cit.* 1986, p. 266.

19 Bristow, *op. cit.* 1996.

20 Dossie, Robert, *The Handmaid to the Arts*, 1st edn. 1758. New edn. printed for A. Millar, W. Law, and R. Cater, London, 1796, vol. II, p. 111.

21 Butcher, William, *Smith's Art of House Painting*, 1st edn., Richard Laurie, London, 1821.

22 Fowler and Cornforth, *op. cit.* 1986, p. 177.

23 Ibid., p. 26.

24 It must be understood that both were written before recent EU legislation restricted the use of lead paint to certain applications.

25 This contravenes the *Lead Paint Regulations* of 1927, which specifically prohibited the dry rubbing down of all painted surfaces other than those of iron- or steelwork, provided that it could be proved that such painted surfaces contained no lead.

26 Fowler and Cornforth, *op. cit.* 1986, p. 177.

27 Ibid.

28 Ibid.

29 Dossie, *op. cit.* 1796, p. 28.

30 Hay, D. R., *The Laws of Harmonious Colouring Adapted to Interior Decorations, with Observations on the Practice of House Painting.* 6th edn., William Blackwood and Sons, Edinburgh and London, 1847, p. 127.

31 See, for example, Jennings, Arthur Seymour, *The Decoration and Renovation of the Home*, W. R. Howell & Company, London, 1924, p. 60.

32 Fowler and Cornforth, *op. cit.* 1986, p. 178.

33 Ibid.

34 Ibid.

35 Hussey, Christopher, *Paint, Colour-Wash and Climbing Plants*, Georgian Pamphlet No. 3, The Georgian Group, London, 1947.

36 Cornforth, *op. cit.* 1985, p. 183.

37 Ibid.

38 Ibid., p. 119.

39 For a brief account of the basic methods of paint analysis see Baty, Patrick, 'The Role of Paint Analysis in the Historic Interior', in *The Journal of Architectural Conservation*, March 1995, pp. 27–37.

40 Bristow, Ian, 'Paint Samples from the Entrance Hall at Kelmarsh', this volume pp. 41–51.

41 Commonly known as 'water paint', or 'oil-bound water paint'.

42 See Chatfield, H. W., *Paint and Varnish Manufacture*, Charles Griffin, London, 1955, pp. 324–5; and Holloway, J. G. E., *The Modern Painter and Decorator*, 5th edn, The Caxton Publishing Company Ltd, London, 1961, vol. I, pp. 131–8.

43 Cornforth, *op. cit.* 1985, p. 183.

44 Ironically, an oil-bound water paint is an emulsion, i.e. a mixture of liquids that will not normally mix together – oil and water. 'Walpamur', the type used so often on his projects, was a product that first appeared in 1906, and a later variant of a type introduced in the 1870s.

45 Cornforth, *op. cit.* 1985, p. 183.

46 Hurst, A. E., *Painting and Decorating*, 8th edn., Charles Griffin, London, 1963, p. 232.

47 Fowler and Cornforth, *op. cit.* 1986, p. 180.

48 Smith, John, *The Art of Painting in Oyl*, 5th edn., 1723, p. 40.

49 Jones, Chester, *Colefax and Fowler: The Best in English Interior Decoration*, Barrie & Jenkins, London, 1989.

50 Ibid., p. 83.

51 Ibid., p. 84.

52 Cornforth, *op. cit.* 1985, p. 184.

53 Gettens, Rutherford J., Kühn, Hermann, and Chase, W. T, 'Lead White' in: Roy, Ashok (ed.), *Artists' Pigments – A Handbook of their Characteristics*, vol. II, National Gallery of Art, Washington, 1993, p. 70, 'Because of its high refractive index, the hiding power of lead white, even in oil is high.'

54 Two examples come to mind. One is the Kirtlington Park Room, now in the Metropolitan Museum of Art, New York, which can be seen in the illustrations on p. 140 of a recent book by Amelia Peck and others, *Period Rooms in the Metropolitan Museum of Art*, Metropolitan Museum of Art, New York, 1996, pp. 137–45.

The other is the recently repainted Long Gallery, at Osterley Park, Middlesex.

55 Dated 10 April 1767, from Rowland Belasis to Lord Fauconberg, who was then remodelling Newburgh Priory in N. Yorkshire.

56 Sir Francis Dashwood, *The Dashwoods of 55 West Wycombe*, Aurum Press, London, 1990.

57 22 Avery Row was the entrance to Nancy Lancaster's private accommodation at the back of the Colefax & Fowler shop on 39 Brook Street.

58 Dashwood, *op. cit.*, 1990 p. 207.

59 Ibid., p. 216.

60 This author was recently asked to carry out paint research in a country house in Wiltshire. Prior to this, scrapes had suggested that three schemes had been applied in the Library – analysis revealed that it had been decorated, or partially decorated, on nine occasions since being built in the 1780s. Similar discrepancies were found in other rooms.

61 Dashwood, *op. cit.*, 1990, p.185.

62 Fowler and Cornforth, *op. cit.* 1986, p. 21.

COLOUR IN HISTORIC HOUSES
IN PUBLIC OWNERSHIP

IAN BRISTOW

THE PURPOSE of this paper is to show that, in parallel with the general development in the British Isles of scholarship in the matter of architectural history, during the mid-twentieth century much of significance was happening in the field of historic interiors that lay beyond the particular milieu of John Fowler. To illustrate this counterpoint to his talents, I will look particularly at a number of country houses and comparable historic buildings in public ownership, where from the 1930s to the 1980s increasingly careful approaches have been made to a stricter authenticity in their redecoration.

Pre-war Background

Rather than looking immediately at the key examples, I must first touch on the background of the decades of Edward VII and George V into which Fowler was born. By the latter part of the nineteenth century, the tenets of colour theory which had been developed from the work of Johann Goethe by George Field, David Ramsay Hay, and Owen Jones (and latterly promulgated by such figures as Christopher Dresser and Ellis A. Davidson) were being questioned and set to one side.[1] On this account, the colour system published by Wilhelm Ostwald in Leipzig in 1916 seems in the present context to have fallen on stony ground;[2] and, while in about 1930 it was popularized in educational circles in England,[3] and a discussion of colour theory was used to inform the modernistic schemes presented by John Holmes in 1931 in his *Colour in Interior Decoration*,[4] such approaches were, it appears, more material to the Modern Movement than to historic interiors.

Accordingly, if one looks at the first book produced by the architect Basil Ionides, *Colour and Interior Decoration* (1926),[5] one finds in his colour-by-colour tables an almost completely subjective analysis. At the same time, the 'two-tones of blue-grey' shown on the panelling in his illustration of the sitting room of the Hon. Lionel Holland (which overlooked the Thames near the Adelphi)[6] relate naturally to the intuitive taste advocated in late nineteenth-century America by Edith Wharton and Ogden Codman, who advised, notably simply, that the fewer the colours used in a room 'the more pleasing and restful the result will be'.

Reflecting the tenets of the Arts and Crafts movement, Wharton and Codman also praised the virtues of 'a really fine old Eastern rug … subtly harmonised by time',[7] another feature of Lionel Holland's room; and this penchant for antique furniture and textiles was met in Britain by a number of firms, notably, particularly in the present connection, Francis Lenygon, who traded from 31 Old Burlington Street from 1909.[8] A book complementing the business was issued under his name in the same year,[9] but was in reality written by Margaret Jourdain, who became the foremost scholar of the Georgian interior in the years around the First World War, and continued to publish until after the Second. Her four large volumes on historic interiors and furnishings remain invaluable today,[10] and no doubt

Figure I The Egyptian
Hall, Mansion House, 1931.
Country Life Picture Library

helped to engender an increasing taste for coloured paint in interiors after the First World War. Thus in 1924 it was said:[11]

> The nineteen-twenties in England have discovered paint and light and are beginning – tentatively, experimentally – to use them.

Supporting this assertion, while in 1923 the polychrome of 1896 by the firm of decorators, Gillows, in the Egyptian Hall at the Mansion House, London, was largely painted out in cream, the scheme by Sydney Tatchell which succeeded it in 1931 was based on cream, gold, and blue.

The ceiling was a 'very full ivory colour' with the central motifs in 'pale sepia' on a background of 'Italian blue'; a 'Grecian Key pattern in blue' was added around these, and the laurel bands were shaded with 'burnt sienna'; the walls, gallery fronts, and columns were of 'Caen-stone' colour of various tones; while the curtains and carpet were blue and gold.[12]

Significantly, Tatchell claimed that his scheme was 'based on the style and period

contemporary with the date of the building', and (leaving aside the fact that the vault was by Dance the younger and dated from 1795–6) it may well have been informed by the painter's account of 1757, which showed that the walls were painted a 'beautiful stone colour'.[13] Tatchell was no doubt familiar with the documentary evidence through the work of his predecessor, Sydney Perks, who in 1922 had published *The History of the Mansion House*, in which reference was made to the relevant documents;[14] and that such detailed research was carried out to provide an understanding of the building's history is important.

Developing interest in documentary studies of seventeenth- and eighteenth-century classical buildings emanated from the days of the Queen Anne movement, and Perks's way had been paved by the publications of several architects, notably J. A. Gotch and Reginald Blomfield, both of whom were active in repair or refurbishment work on buildings of the period. A contemporary view of the interior of Batsford's bookshop, where both new and second-hand volumes were for sale, aptly illustrates the often embryonic scholarship of the day;[15] while added impetus was undoubtedly lent to study and research by the work to secure the dome of St Paul's Cathedral in the first half of the 1920s,[16] the published fruits of which are to be seen most obviously in the volumes of the Wren Society.

In today's context, the vital project of the inter-war years was, of course, the restoration in 1934–5 of Inigo Jones's Queen's House at Greenwich under the direction of George Chettle of the Office of Works. Against a background of the scholarship of Gotch, W. Grant Keith, and Geoffrey Callender, Chettle made dedicated documentary studies of the building, extending from the limited manuscript accounts of the Jones period through to those of the early eighteenth century. The results are incorporated into the fourteenth monograph of the *Survey of London* (1937), in which Chettle said of the house after completion of the repair work:[17]

Its past splendours cannot be given back to it in full, but at least hints of them have been revealed. Its rooms once more show the dignity of their planning and the beauty of their proportion, and once more their walls are hung with pictures.

In terms of painted decoration, the most notable discoveries were the blue and gold scheme in the room which he called the Queen's Drawing Room or Queen's Cabinet,[18] and the gilded scheme in the Hall, which was uncovered from beneath 24 overlying coats of paint 'with infinite patience and skill by the artists in the service of H. M. Office of Works'.[19]

Leaving aside the destruction of the 1662 alterations to the first-floor rooms on the park side,[20] and although the aged 'grey-green' background (which Chettle seems to have accepted without question) had in fact started life as white,[21] the whole exercise represents a remarkable achievement for its day. Standing squarely in the scholarly tradition of the Office of Works and Ancient Monuments Board, it is notable for the careful combination of documentary and physical investigative work that informed it.

Two other elements of the background to

the Queen's House project must also be mentioned: the research work concurrently proceeding at Colonial Williamsburg, with which I believe Chettle may have had some experience; and the contemporary attempts to return the interior of the Royal Pavilion at Brighton to its Regency state.

Apropos the latter, writing in 1939 Henry D. Roberts indicated that the opportunity had been taken, during repairs being carried out in the mid-1920s after the building's occupation during the First World War as a military hospital, to remove some of the paintwork and decoration executed since acquisition of the building in 1850 by the town of Brighton, and to expose as much as possible of the earlier work. The object was, he said, to continue the process:[22]

> … in such a way that all the rooms may so be restored that their appearance will be nearer to what it was when the Pavilion was a Royal residence.

What had been achieved by 1909 was, in fact, quite limited but besides the return of a few items of furniture and memorabilia from Buckingham Palace, in 1934 the pilasters were restored to the Saloon, and in 1938 part of the Chinese wallpaper.[23]

Figure 2 (left) The Hall, Queen's House, Greenwich. *Greenwich Maritime Museum Photographic Library*

Figure 3 (right) View of the Saloon in the Royal Pavilion, Brighton, 1939. *Royal Pavilion and Museums, Brighton and Hove*

Nevertheless, it is important that in preparing for this Roberts undertook a significant amount of documentary research into the original interior decorations.

Post-war Developments

Surrounding these research-led projects lay, however, the comforting world of the interior decorator. Before the War, the American heiress Nancy Tree (a niece of Lady Astor) had been 'helped' by a number of leading figures, including Mrs Bethel (for the grander rooms at Kelmarsh in the second half of the 1920s); Syrie Maugham (for her temporary residence at the Home Farm during the time Ditchley was being renovated in the first half of the 1930s); and (for the main house itself) the French decorator Stéphane Boudin.[24]

After this period of gestation, it was the second half of the 1940s which saw the birth of the so-called 'English Country-House Style' through the liaison of Nancy Lancaster (as, through remarriage, she now became) with John Fowler, who had been working for Sibyl Colefax since about 1938. Between them, from her acquisition of the firm at about the beginning of 1947, they developed the business, each with their own eye for style. Nancy Lancaster provided the capital, contacts, clientele, and a cosmopolitan perspective on design (besides a firm steer on the standards of comfort which, through the reputation of her pre-war renovations, the moneyed classes had now come to expect), while John Fowler, with his theatrical background and interest in textiles, wallpapers, and the decorative arts (much of which had been gained by study at the Victoria & Albert Museum) produced the immaculately finished goods.[25]

The heady wine of the *assemblage* can be seen with particular clarity in Mrs Lancaster's two post-war town houses, firstly at 18a Charles Street, the address where she lived from 1945 to 1957. Here, no doubt partly through the exigencies of retrenchment from her larger pre-war establishments, the comforts of the first-floor Drawing Room spilled out on to the landing in the form of a sofa and drinks cupboard; while a decor of distinctly neo-Regency drawing-room style, including striped wallpaper, a quasi-tented ceiling, and framed black silhouettes, flowed down the stairs into the entrance hall.[26] When she moved to 22 Avery Row in 1957,[27] an even more intense vestibule was created from the former servants' entrance, employing marbling, serried prints of Medici portraits, and a banquette too narrow for sitting on, placed between opposed mirrors.

The whole is a pure stage set, based on the poetic art of allusion, and has been described by her biographer both as resembling a Venetian villa and as giving the impression of a royal cabinet.[28] While, undoubtedly, 'showcases of the fantastic possibilities of interior decoration',[29] both rooms completely negate the eighteenth-century view of appropriateness of decor, which is today increasingly understood;[30] but at the time they met in full measure the needs of the post-war age for reference to grander times, houses, people, friends, and relatives.

What then of public architecture during this era? Leaving aside the need to repair (often under the auspices of the War Damage Commission) such important landmarks as St James's Piccadilly, Trinity House, or the Navy Staircase at Somerset House (all instances in which Albert Richardson acted as architect), for today perhaps the most vital public project undertaken by the Ministry of Works was Chiswick House, ravaged by dry rot through lack of maintenance and languishing low down in the order of priorities. While today there is no doubt that (at considerable expense, both in terms of money and architectural legibility) the 1788 wing would have been retained, I myself am glad that the core of the building, originally built as a detached pavilion to a Jacobean house, was given its true *mise en valeur*. Here, in the early 1950s, both George Chettle (already encountered at the Queen's House) and Patrick Faulkner were involved; and while it

Figure 4 Tetrastyle Hall at Marble Hill. *English Heritage Photographic Library*

seems few details of any documentary research are recorded, I assume that (wanting the scholarship of such doyens of the current era as John Harris and Richard Hewlings[31]) restoration to the original form was at least based on the plans and elevations published in William Kent's *The Works of Inigo Jones*.[32]

That this was complemented by careful examination of the structure was made clear by Patrick Faulkner in a conversation on site a few years ago, when he drew my attention in particular to the scratch marks made on the floor of the Red Velvet Room by the original dado-high doors in the destroyed Venetian window, which allowed the precise centres of their hinges to be determined. On colour, samples I have taken for English Heritage have confirmed (with two minor exceptions) the accurate reinstatement of the blue and gold scheme in the Blue Velvet Room, and the verbatim overpainting of the white on those parts of the white and gold ceiling and entablature in the Red Velvet Room which survived before repair; although it must be said that the investigative techniques of the day had led to fundamental misinterpretation of the scheme in the Octagonal Saloon.[33]

At the time, presentation of the interior was hampered by lack of the original furniture (although, as pioneered at the Brighton Pavilion, this is now being increasingly remedied); and the same pertained at Marble Hill, where, again following the ravages of water ingress and resulting dry rot, a notable rescue was effected in the mid-1960s under the auspices of the London County Council.

Here, the background research by Marie Draper and W. A. Eden was squarely set in the scholarly tradition of the *Survey of London* and, by informing the painstaking examination of the fabric and hence the repair programme, presented a model of its kind. As so commonly, however, other than as suggested by some of the room names in the 1767 inventory,[34] nothing specific was found about the colours used and recourse was had to the investigative technique of the day (here described as 'an oblique section through successive coats of paint').[35] Apart from the Great Room, which was found to have been white, this exercise showed the general joinery colour to have been 'a light stone colour in which there was a tinge of green', although it was not possible to secure 'an accurate indication of the depth and

Figure 5 The Palladio Room, Clandon. *National Trust Photographic Library*

intensity of the tonal values'. In redecoration, therefore, these were 'necessarily a matter of judgement' and 'varied according to the aspect of the room in question'.[36] Recently I have been able to refine the investigation and quantify the colour more accurately, both in Lady Suffolk's Bedchamber, and in the Tetrastyle Hall, where in fact two colours were used, one greenish and the other warmer in tone.[37]

Similar problems of lack of evidence and historically associated furniture were faced by the National Trust at Clandon and Sudbury in the late 1960s, and John Fowler was employed to pull the interiors together. At Clandon, the removal of the state bed from the Green Drawing Room to the original State Bedroom was prompted by the 1778 inventory (Inskip p. 7, Figures 8 and 9); but in his account of the work, perhaps because further documentary input was lacking, John Cornforth mentions none. Physical investigation, however, allowed the discovery of early wallpapers, which were copied; and in the Saloon what was believed to be the original colour scheme on the ceiling and entablature was exposed, and the walls repainted on the basis of 'scrapes' (Inskip p. 5, Knox p. 16, Sitwell p. 28).

Otherwise the solution seems to have been based on Fowler's design sense.

In the Palladio Room, in particular, John Cornforth notes that the colouring used to tie the ceiling and wallpaper together was part of a non-historical solution; while in the Saloon the doors were painted out in the varied beiges which were one of Fowler's hallmarks, on the grounds that they were mahogany of a 'Victorian fiery red' which was 'out of tone'.[38]

At Sudbury, John Cornforth mentions no documentary input; and while Fowler wanted to keep existing schemes of decoration in several of the interiors, he notes that colour and pattern were used elsewhere '… to create a sense of progression in the house and make up for the bareness of most of the rooms'. Similarly, gilding was added in the Saloon 'to give more definition'.[39]

John Fowler's first project for the National Trust had been at Claydon in 1956–7; and, as John Cornforth has asserted, it was 'a bold step' for the Trust to employ a decorator.[40] Considering this, one must not forget the pressures the Trust had been under. In 1945, for instance, John Piper had questioned how '… if such a fate should meet it' Seaton Delaval '… would deal with

Figure 6 (left) The Round Gallery, Ham House following the recreation of the 1630s colour scheme in 1979 (now overpainted).

Figure 7 (right) The Saloon of the Casino at Marino, Dublin, redecorated in its original colour scheme c. 1773.

consignment to the National Trust', suggesting it '... might cause the veteran to split its sides with disastrous laughter' and praying 'May its surrounding grass never be mowed by the smooth Atco';[41] while in January the same year Sir Osbert Sitwell noted the passing of the great English houses as '... being wrecked by happy and eager planners, or becoming sterilised and scionless possessions of the National Trust'.[42]

One must accordingly understand the strongly perceived need to avoid a museum-like atmosphere, and in visual terms the results produced by John Fowler for the National Trust were undoubtedly warmer and more polished than those seen at the same time in such houses as the Queen's House, Chiswick, and Marble Hill. In truth, however, by the late 1960s Fowler's undoubted talent for and fascination with the subject were increasingly challenged by the more objective attitudes developing in the study of architectural history, as evidenced by the debate over his treatment of the seventeenth-century joinery of the staircase at Sudbury, which he painted white.[43] (Knox p.17, Figures 6 and 7) The rights and wrongs of the matter are today shrouded in the obscurity of carefully chosen words, but in the light of developing work on room usage and hierarchy (which notably came together in 1978, the year after Fowler's death, in Mark Girouard's *Life in the English Country House*[44]) the associated yellow walls must surely strike an inappropriate note.

Of all the official appointments of the period, one of the most far-reaching was demonstrably that of Peter Thornton as Keeper of Furniture and Woodwork at the Victoria & Albert Museum in 1966. The previous year he had published his important study *Baroque and Rococo Silks*,[45] but had also had experience of restoration and furnishing projects in Denmark, where Tove Clemmenson was his mentor.[46] The substantial benefits of this were brought to his responsibilities for the interiors of Ham House and Osterley Park, whose associated contemporary furniture had come into public ownership and the

Figure 8 The Green Pavilion, Frogmore House 1990. *The Royal Collection* © *Her Majesty Queen Elizabeth II*

care of the V&A Museum in the late 1940s, while the houses themselves were maintained by the Ministry of Works on 999-year leases from the National Trust.

At both houses, Peter and his colleagues embarked on a comprehensive programme of documentary research; at Ham, for example, they were able to re-establish most of its seventeenth-century furniture (which represents a quite extraordinary survival) not only in its original rooms, but even in many instances in the proper location within them. This involved study of the seventeenth-century accounts for the two main phases of alteration, together with the three seventeenth-century inventories.[47] Using these the interior decoration was reviewed, and tactful input increasingly made towards better-considered decisions. The high point was surely the restoration in 1979 of the immensely important, documented blue and gold scheme of 1637–8 in the Round Gallery following technical research by Jo Darrah of the Museum's Department of Conservation, providing a remarkable model of interdisciplinary coordination and setting a new standard of objectivity.[48]

I, of course, owe much to Jo for all her

help in 1975–8 when I held my research fellowship at York; and one of the first projects to which I was able to bring its rich harvest was the restoration of the original scheme of decoration by William Chambers in the Saloon and other rooms at the Casino, Marino, Dublin, where my clients were the Office of Public Works. Here, documentary evidence located by John Harris, Cynthia O'Connor, and John Redmill was combined with paint sampling and other physical investigation; and, while there were no historically associated contents, I believe this, complemented by the use of authentically formulated lead paint, took a further step to a better understanding of true historic aesthetics.[49]

The crowning public-sector achievement of the 1980s, however, was the redecoration of much of the interior at Frogmore. The house dates from 1680 and is attributed to Hugh May, but was completely refitted inside in the 1790s by James Wyatt for Queen Charlotte, while the decor was further developed over successive phases during the nineteenth-century occupations of Princess Augusta and the Duchess of Kent. Here not only did documentary evidence abound, much of it in the form of water-colours and early photographs, but also many of the historically associated contents. Very many people were involved with research, planning, investigation, and execution, either within the Property Services Agency (PSA), the Directorate of Ancient Monuments and Historic Buildings (later English Heritage), the Royal Household, or as external consultants; and I believe the project set a wholly new standard, showing how much stronger is an intimate combination of careful investigation and aesthetic sense, than the latter unsupported.[50]

In this connection, it is particularly notable that all the colours I determined were reproduced verbatim, without any need for editing on grounds of taste.[51] Indeed, one of the great lessons I have learned is that one has to trust the aesthetic abilities of the great figures of the past, just as much in terms of colour as in architectural form. Thus in the staircase, James Wyatt's pale green found its natural place on the walls; and in the Green Pavilion, the green seen in W. H. Pyne's illustration of a year or two before 1820 was identified through paint sampling, and directly reproduced as an authentic part of the decor.[52] In the Colonnade, I have to say we nearly lost our nerve, since the warm stone colour found on the walls appeared on a small sample very weak compared with that shown on the remarkable coloured-up photograph of 1861,[53] but once applied, proved to be exactly right. In the Mary Moser Room, by contrast, the mid-nineteenth-century decor survived in a fairly intact state, and a more conservative approach was accordingly adopted, with many paint surfaces simply being cleaned and touched in.

Since 1990, when Frogmore was opened to the public on a regular basis, the Property Sevices Agency has been abolished, and the splinters of its baton passed to a number of separately constituted bodies. Also, the field of historic interiors has proved an amazing growth industry, with a strongly flowing tide of historic-colour ranges, reproduction fabrics, and wallpapers, some of fair quality

in their authenticity, but others, one has to say, of lesser merit.

In what has necessarily been the slightest sketch of developments from the 1930s to the 1980s, I have had to omit mention of many projects and individuals (I think particularly of the conservation of the Thornhill decor in the Painted Hall at Greenwich, redecoration of the Adam interiors at Culzean Castle by Rab Snowden of the Stenhouse Conservation Centre in Edinburgh, restoration of the Adam colours by the Greater London Council in the Library at Kenwood, and Ian Gow's work in the late 1970s at Audley End); while there are undoubtedly some less successful essays over which a veil is best drawn. I hope however that, although it has often been swamped by the popular myths of the twentieth-century 'country-house style', I have been able to make evident an unsung line of academic development in the approach to redecoration, and show how important the technical work and scholarship brought to bear on buildings in public ownership has been in setting new standards of objectivity. Having met John Fowler on two occasions through the good offices of John Cornforth, I like to think he would have been the first to appreciate the broader knowledge-base of today; and my hope for the future is that by further educating the eye of the public in the understanding of true historic aesthetics, the twenty-first century will see an ever more appropriate and sympathetic use of colour in buildings on public display.

References

1 Bristow, Ian C., 'Colour theory in the mid-19th century', in Airs, Malcolm (ed.), *The Victorian Great House*, Oxford University Press, Oxford, 2000, p. 105.
2 Ostwald, Wilhelm, *Die Farbenfibel*, Verlag Unesma, Leipzig, 1916.
3 Ostwald, Wilhelm, *Colour Science*, authorized translation by J. Scott Taylor, 1931–3, Windsor and Newton, London.
4 Holmes, John, *Colour in Interior Decoration*, Architectural Press, London; Charles Scribner's Sons, New York, 1931.
5 Ionides, Basil, *Colour and Interior Decoration*,

Country Life, London, 1926.

6 Ibid, p. 38, pl. vii.

7 Wharton, Edith and Codman, Ogden, *The Decoration of Houses*, B.T. Batsford, 1898 reprint of the original 1897 edition, pp. 28–9.

8 Cornforth, John, *The Inspiration of the Past: Country House Taste in the Twentieth Century*, Viking, London, 1985, p. 48.

9 Lenygon, Francis, *The Decoration and Furniture of English Mansions during the Seventeenth and Eighteenth Centuries* T. Werner Laurie, London, 1909.

10 Jourdain, Margaret, *Decoration in England from 1660 to 1770*, B.T. Batsford, London, 1914; *Furniture in England from 1660–1760*, B.T. Batsford, London, 1914; *English Decoration and Furniture of the later XVIIIth Century (1760–1820)*, B.T. Batsford, London, 1922; *English Decoration and Furniture of the Early Renaissance*, B.T. Batsford, London, 1924. Note: the first two volumes were published under the pseudonym of Francis Lenygon.

11 *The Smaller House*, Architectural Press, London, 1924, p. v.

12 Jeffery, Sally, *The Mansion House*, Phillimore, London, 1993, pp. 242, 244, 256.

13 Ibid., pp.139, 233ff, 256.

14 Perks, Sydney, *The History of the Mansion House*, Cambridge University Press, Cambridge, 1922, p. 192.

15 Pamphlet in author's possession.

16 Alexander, S. A., *The Safety of St. Paul's*, 1927; Harvey, William, *The Preservation of St. Paul's Cathedral*, Architectural Press, London, 1925.

17 Chettle, George H., *The Queen's House, Greenwich*, 14th Monograph of the London Survey Committee, 1937, p. 58.

18 Ibid., pp. 69–71, pl. 60.

19 Ibid., pp. 64–5, pls. 39–41.

20 Ormond, Richard, and others, 'The Queen's House, Greenwich', in *ASCHB Transactions 1989*, vol.14, 1990, p. 10 (section by Harold Yexley, 'Scope and Design of the Project').

21 Bristow, Ian C., 'Interior Paintwork', in Airs, Malcolm (ed.) *The Seventeenth Century Great House*, University of Oxford, Oxford, 1995, p. 109. See also: Ormond, Richard, and others, *op. cit.* 1990 (section by Bristow, Ian C., 'Reconstruction of the Historic Paint Colours').

22 Roberts, Henry D., *A History of the Royal Pavilion Brighton*, Country Life, London, 1939, pp. 209–10.

23 Ibid., pp. 141, 144, 148, 149, 212.

24 Becker, Robert, *Nancy Lancaster: Her Life, Her World, Her Art*, Alfred A. Knopf, New York, 1998 edition (first published 1996), pp. 157–8, 201, 203, 204–5, 270.

25 Ibid., pp. 304–12; Cornforth, *op. cit.* 1985, pp. 144, 157.

26 Becker, *op. cit.* 1998, p. 316, illustrated p. 319.

27 22 Avery Row was the entrance to Nancy Lancaster's private accommodation at the back of the Colefax & Fowler shop on 39 Brook Street.

28 Becker, *op. cit.*, 1998, pp. 321–2.

29 Ibid., p. 320.

30 Bristow, Ian C., *Architectural Colour in British Interiors 1615–1840*, Yale University Press, New Haven and London, 1996, p.198; Watkin, David, *Sir John Soane, Enlightenment Thought and the Royal Academy Lectures*, Cambridge University Press, Cambridge, 1996, pp. 196ff.

31 Harris, John, *The Palladian Revival: Lord Burlington, His Villa and Garden at Chiswick*, Yale University Press, New Haven, 1994; Hewlings, Richard, 'Chiswick House and Gardens; Appearance and Meaning' in Barnard, Toby and Clark, Jane (eds.), *Lord Burlington: Architecture, Art and Life*, Hambledon, London, 1995, pp. 1–149.

32 Kent, William, *The Works of Inigo Jones*, William Kent, London, 1727, pls. 70–3.

33 Bristow, Ian C., ongoing investigations: 'Chiswick House, Middlesex: Report on an investigation of paint samples from the Blue Velvet Room (final draft)', March 1990, revised September 1991; 'Chiswick House, Middlesex: Report on an investigation of paint samples from the Octagonal Saloon (final draft)', March 1990, revised November 1996; 'Chiswick House, Middlesex: Report on an investigation of paint samples from the Red Velvet Room and the Venetian window in the Gallery (preliminary submission)', August 1991.

34 Draper, Marie P. G. and Eden, F. C., *Marble Hill House and its Owners*, Greater London Council, London, 1970, p. 27.

35 Ibid., p. 57.

36 Ibid., pp. 31, 57.

37 Bristow, Ian C., 'Marble Hill, Middlesex: Report on an investigation of paint samples from Lady Suffolk's Bedchamber', March 1997; 'Marble Hill, Middlesex: Report on an investigation of paint samples from the Tetrastyle Hall', March 1997.

38 Cornforth, *op. cit.* 1985, pp. 217–18 (for reference to 'scrapes' see Fowler, John and Cornforth, John, *English Decoration in the 18th Century*, Barrie & Jenkins, London, 1974, caption to pl. XXVII).

39 Cornforth, *op. cit.* 1985, pp. 212–13.

40 Ibid., pp. 200, 213.

41 Piper, John, *Building and Prospects*, Architectural Press, London 1948, pp. 87–8.

42 Cornforth, *op. cit.* 1985, p. 86 (citing Sir Osbert Sitwell in the introduction to his exhibition *The Sitwell Country* at the Leicester Galleries, January 1945).

43 Ibid., p. 213.

44 Girouard, Mark, *Life in the English Country House*, Yale University Press, 1978.

45 Thornton, Peter, *Baroque and Rococo Silks*, MacDonald, London, 1965.

46 See Clemmenson, Tove and Raabyemagle, Hanne, *Brede Hovedbygning 1795–1806*, Nationalmuseet, Copenhagen, 1996.

47 Thornton, Peter and Tomlin, Maurice, *The Decoration and Furnishing of Ham House*, Furniture History Society, 1980.

48 Darrah, Josephine, MS. Notebooks in Department of Conservation, Victoria & Albert Museum, vol.1, p. 27, samples 4–20 (samples stored at ibid. and exposure tests still (2001) visible on back of door to staircase). For an illustration of the reconstructed scheme before obliteration, see Bristow, *op. cit.* 1996, fig. 24.

49 Redmill, John and Bristow, Ian C., 'The Casino at Marino, Dublin', *ASCHB Transactions*, vol. 9, 1984, pp. 29–44.

50 Cornforth, John, 'Frogmore House, Berkshire', in *Country Life*, vol. clxxxiv no. 33, 16 August 1990, pp. 46–51; vol. clxxxiv no 34, 23 August 1980, pp. 42–5.

51 Bristow, Ian C. 'Frogmore House, Berkshire: Report on an investigation of paint samples for the Property Services Agency, Department of the Environment', February 1986.

52 Pyne, W. H., *History of the Royal Residences*, 1819, Vol. i, Frogmore, p. 13 (the original watercolour is in the Royal Library at Windsor, no. 22121).

53 Royal Library, Windsor, ref. S. A., vol. i p. 7(d).

JOHN FOWLER AND NANCY LANCASTER AT KELMARSH HALL

MARIANNE SÜHR

I WRITE THIS article not as a paint expert, nor as a great John Fowler enthusiast, but simply as a Surveyor to the Fabric of a little-known country house in Northamptonshire. Little known, that is, until quite recently. The house is Kelmarsh Hall.

Kelmarsh Hall was designed by the seminal architect James Gibbs, and the house plans and elevations were published in his *A Book of Architecture* in 1728. However, over the last few years interest in the house has focused less on the original architect, and more on its tenant, Nancy Lancaster, a gregarious Virginian woman who came to Kelmarsh exactly 200 years later. It is becoming increasingly apparent that her involvement at Kelmarsh played a pivotal role in twentieth-century interior decoration.

Nancy Lancaster, then married to Ronnie Tree, moved in 1928 to Kelmarsh, where they agreed to redecorate the Hall in lieu of

Figure 1 Nancy Lancaster at Haseley Court, June 1960. *Photograph by courtesy of Cecil Beaton Studio Archive, Sotheby's*

rent. This appears to be Nancy's first major project in England, and where she really developed her style and experimented with ideas. Her work at Kelmarsh was a springboard for her later career; it was featured widely in society journals such as *Country Life*, and in time became a source of inspiration for John Fowler.

Nancy, by all accounts, was quite a remarkable character. Michael Astor described her personality in the most glowing terms. He said:[1]

> She brought into a room a flavour of another more exciting world, of what I thought of as 'fast' women and 'worldly' men, who lived uninhibited lives and were forever concerned with ethics, and whom I felt I could get along with.

The dusty, mothballed interiors at Kelmarsh still hold something of that magic, a magic that cannot be recreated by the clever placing of furniture or the anecdotes of a room steward. At Kelmarsh, the atmosphere of this unrestored and unconsciously presented house still almost hangs in the air.

We believed that the best surviving Nancy Lancaster interior at Kelmarsh was the Entrance Hall. The proportions and details of the room were virtually as Gibbs had designed them, and can be checked against his original drawings, which survive at the RIBA. Nancy said that when she agreed to lease Kelmarsh, 'it had barely been touched'. But houses don't stand still, and Kelmarsh had certainly been no exception. The mellow stippled shades of pink are now flaking to reveal all the schemes of the intervening years.

Originally, the walls appear to have been finished in a very fine, undecorated, burnished plaster, probably mixed with marble dust, to give the impression of a marble-clad Italianate courtyard. This has always proved to be a troublesome substrate. Its smoothness and lack of key meant that subsequent layers of paint never stuck particularly well, and as a result, the room had been frequently redecorated. We spotted vestiges of reds and greens, typical of the nineteenth century, beneath the present scheme.

We know that Nancy painted over a dingy Victorian green scheme in the Hall sometime between 1928 when she took residence and 1933 when *Country Life* featured

Figure 2 (left) The Entrance Hall, Kelmarsh Hall, 1999. *E. Perry.*

Figure 3 (right) Wall of Entrance Hall, Kelmarsh Hall, 1999. *English Heritage.*

Figure 4 (left) The Entrance Hall at Kelmarsh Hall. View of the ceiling and upper walls. *E. Perry*

Figure 5 (right) The Entrance Hall at Kelmarsh Hall. Detail of flaking paint and texture of scheme, 1999. *English Heritage*

the house. In Robert Becker's biography of Nancy Lancaster, he quotes her as saying:[2]

> I painted the hall at Kelmarsh pink, I never thought twice about using bright colors in an old house. The pink I used was an Italian pink, a light terracotta. The idea came from Lady Islington's house, Rushbrooke Hall… Anne Islington was the person in England who had the very best taste and the very best color sense… [she] allowed me to send Kick [Nancy's decorator] to Rushbrooke to analyze the pink so that I might reproduce it. When he was finished, the effect of the room was breathtaking… I had two chairs covered in the most wonderful tangerine velvet, another in emerald green, one Queen Anne wing chair in bright yellow brocade and a chair and a sofa in striped fabric I bought in Italy.
>
> Then filled the hall with the three things that were essential to me in any room: real candle light, wood fires and lovely flowers. Those were my tricks.

Today we can only use our imagination to feel the colours, but Nancy's description brings the black and white *Country Life* photograph to life.

We were all very excited at the prospect of having a real Nancy Lancaster scheme at Kelmarsh. It got even better when a builder who was working at the Hall was at the pub with a chap who was working for a lady down the road who knew the decorator who applied the actual paint. The decorator's name, discovered by complete accident, was Ken Cowens.

We invited Ken to the Hall to see if he could shed any further light on the work. It turns out that he redecorated the Hall not in 1928 but in 1950. He remembers the date as he had to leave early one day because his

wife went into labour. But our hopes of an original Nancy Lancaster interior were not lost. By 1950, Nancy had divorced Ronnie Tree, with whom she had originally rented Kelmarsh, and married Colonel Lancaster, who was, rather fortuitously, its owner. By this time Nancy had bought Sibyl Colefax Ltd, an established interior decoration firm. Nancy made John Fowler a partner (previously he was just an employee), and changed the name to Colefax & Fowler. She was herself going through a name change at the time, and I suppose 'Tree Fowler' was an unfortunate combination and didn't quite conjure up the same pleasant associations.

But here the problem starts. Ken's memory was superb, but he had no recollection of Nancy Lancaster ever visiting during the redecorations of 1950. He said that Betty Guinness was a regular guest of Colonel Lancaster, but not Nancy. The local Women's Institute (WI) register was an excellent source of information, and provided information about when Nancy was at Kelmarsh, as she would regularly attend meetings. This helped us piece together which projects were under Nancy's supervision and which may have been carried out in her absence. But the WI records were not looking good.

Ken Cowens does remember, however, John Fowler coming up from London to cast a designer's eye over the work. Ken explained that Fowler sent his own colour mixer, Horace, to work with the local firm. He is quite definite that no effort was made to copy the earlier colour. We know that around this period, Nancy and Colonel Lancaster were corresponding through their solicitors, and that she and John Fowler had

had a falling out. So Nancy's involvement in the present scheme is unclear.

As a consequence of our meeting Ken, there has been some considerable dispute about the significance of the present scheme. The optimists, and Fowler fans, suggest it is a wonderful example of a great patron, Nancy Lancaster, working in conjunction with a great designer, John Fowler, in a house that led the way for cutting-edge interior design. Others may argue that it was an economical cheering up after the Second World War, applied by a local decorator, colour-mixed by a chap named Horace, vaguely under the direction of John Fowler at a time when he and Nancy were not even speaking. The latter scenario places the real significance firmly with the earlier, pre-1933 scheme.

When considering a treatment for the decoration of the Hall today, a number of practical problems have to be addressed. In patches, the paint is not properly adhered to the substrate. At best it is severely crazed, at worst it is flaking off and exposing the white ground or earlier colours beneath. So, even if we can agree that the present scheme is of primary significance, the treatment of it is by no means clear-cut.

Our definition of significance requires clarification. We must first wrestle with the questions: what is it that is significant about this scheme? Is it the actual paint layer, the physical presence of the soft distemper glaze over the Walpamur ground? If it is, do we treat it like a medieval wall painting and attempt to conserve it *in situ*? Or rather have we got this whole significance thing wrong?

Compare it to the Penguin Pool at London Zoo in Regent's Park, designed by Lubetkin. When the concrete crumbled because of the corroding reinforcement inside, did we conserve the pieces? No – because the significance was in the architectural concept, the cleanness of the lines, and the overall form, rather than in the fabric. Maybe by attempting to retain the paint at Kelmarsh, we are failing to conserve that thing that is really significant, and that's the concept.

Figure 6 The Entrance Hall, Kelmarsh Hall, Nancy Lancaster scheme 1928–33. *Country Life Picture Library, 1933*

Becker, Nancy's biographer, says about the Hall:[3]

> Here was the mood of the place in one room, unhesitatingly welcoming, absolutely surprising, unashamedly elegant; a rich but fresh setting made from the melding of textures and colours.

The freshness, the life of the Hall, that intangible thing we call ambience or atmosphere, the 'shabby chic' – is it just possible that sometimes, in our great efforts to conserve, we completely miss the point?

We consulted experts. First, the paint experts: Ian Bristow analysed the paint layers and Helen Hughes came to examine the scheme. The archaeology contained within the layers was fascinating – nearly three centuries of colour schemes and paint types. This was important stuff, a physical record of the history of the Hall.

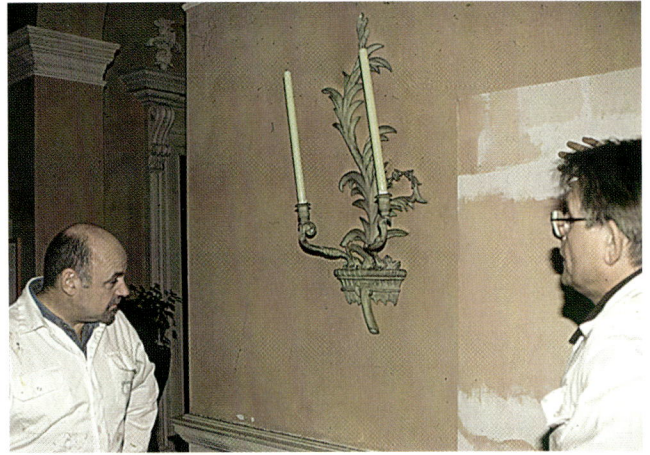

Figure 7 (left) Applying the final glaze over white ground. *Paul Ferraby*

Figure 8 (right) Completed test panel compared to original 1950s decoration. *Paul Ferraby*

We then consulted the plaster experts. It's easy to forget, amidst the Nancy fervour, that the plaster was designed by Gibbs and executed by the Atari Brothers. Of course this would probably have been decorated for the first few decades with a soft distemper and washed off prior to each redecoration to prevent any build-up of paint – but more recent paints have clogged the detail and completely obscured the crispness of the work. So the plaster experts were adamant that the paint should be removed. In practical terms, if we redecorated, we would have to remove the paint in any case in order to get back to a decent substrate.

So, confused and undecided, we rang up Ken again. We needed to test our options.

We needed to find out whether, if we chose to redecorate, we could actually recreate the scheme with any degree of accuracy. Ken kindly agreed to join Tom Greening and Frank Garbutt of the decorating firm Greenings, to put his memory to the test. Ken gave me a shopping list over the phone, which I relayed to Tom and Frank.

Ken firmly stated that no attempt was made to copy Nancy Lancaster's original scheme. Before the present scheme was applied most of the pre-1933 pink glaze was washed off using warm water exposing the original white ground layer. The wall surface was then stopped up and sanded down in preparation for painting. As rationing was still in operation and paint was still under

Figure 9 Nancy's bedroom at Kelmarsh. *Country Life Picture Library*

Figure 10 The Saloon, Kelmarsh. *Country Life Picture Library, 1933*

licence, only one coat of white Walpamur was applied to the walls. The final glaze, a dilute soft distemper (whiting and rabbit-skin glue) mixed with linseed oil and tinted with red sienna, yellow ochre, and burnt umber was applied and stippled with a soft brush.

We spread dust sheets over the floor of the Hall, and following Ken's instructions we attempted to recreate the 1950s scheme on test panels. Tom and Frank set to work and remarkably produced a test panel which matched the 1950s paint exactly – Ken's memory was spot on.

It was Ken who suggested what is probably the best solution so far: to redecorate the lower half of the walls up to the string course – this is where the eye would pick out any defects, and where the walls have suffered the most damage – and then to leave the paint above with all its archaeology.

If you're quick, you might get to see the Hall before it is redecorated, and catch a whiff of the magic that's still present. Whether it will still be there after redecoration is anybody's guess, but it certainly won't be achieved simply through a scientific recreation of the physical conditions.

Of course, Nancy was the real star of Kelmarsh. And I suspect that her early work

at this little-known country house was to have had a great influence on John Fowler. He features the Kelmarsh interiors in the introduction to his book, written with John Cornforth, *English Decoration in the 18th Century.* Fowler describes Nancy's own bedroom at Kelmarsh:[4]

> … the walls were hung with ivory coloured silk and the bed was hung with cloth of silver trimmed with eighteenth-century silver galloon and fringe probably found in Italy … It is only the tiger skin rug in front of the fire and the rather bare walls that give away the date of this room …when one looks again at the photographs taken in 1933, it is hard to believe that they are of rooms arranged and decorated over 40 years ago, or conversely, it is hard to see why they were so novel at the time.

And he goes on to say:[5]

> Mrs Lancaster, although never a professional like Mrs Bethell, Syrie Maugham or Lady Colefax, should be mentioned in their company as one of the key people in the development of English taste in decoration during the last two generations.

Nancy's style was, and is, enduring and timeless. I stumbled upon a copy of *Homes and Gardens* magazine from 1960 in an old cardboard box at Kelmarsh. Following a lavish description of Nancy's Yellow Drawing Room at Brook Street,[6] the article closes by saying: 'such is the barest outline of what must surely be one of the most beautiful and remarkable rooms in London' (Ward p. 69, Figure 6). The room still exists, now as a showroom for Colefax & Fowler. And her style continues, not necessarily through the firm she started, but through her influence on the wider public. I challenge anyone to find a contemporary interiors magazine today that doesn't contain a tiger-skin rug.

Robert Becker, in his biography of Nancy, came up with an interesting idea. He wrote: 'Perhaps it was the inherent beauty of the country house milieu that allowed the trappings of a past age to outlive the inventors.' This suggestion was confirmed to me a couple of years ago, in a dentist's waiting room

in Westbury-on-Trym. I was flicking through the pages of a cheap magazine when I came across this. The article starts with a definitive statement, which I quote: 'The creator of the quintessential English country house style was an American, Nancy Lancaster'.

References

1 Astor, Micheal, Tribal Feeling: A Study of the Astor Family, Murray, London, 1963, pp. 79–80.
2 Becker, Robert, Nancy Lancaster: Her Life, Her World, Her Art, Alfred A. Knopf, New York, 1996, p. 161.
3 Ibid., p. 161.
4 Cornforth, John and Fowler, John, English Decoration in the 18th Century, Barrie & Jenkins, London, 1974, p. 18.
5 Ibid., p. 18.
6 22 Avery Row was the entrance to Nancy Lancaster's private accommodation at the back of the Colefax & Fowler shop on 39 Brook Street.

PAINT SAMPLES FROM THE ENTRANCE HALL AT KELMARSH

IAN BRISTOW

KELMARSH WAS designed by James Gibbs and erected between 1728 and 1732, although only the Entrance Hall and the staircase survive later alterations.[1] In discussing the cross sections taken from the Entrance Hall in May 1999, I must first thank my clients, Colefax & Fowler, who asked me to examine the paintwork and provided me with relevant documentary material from their archive. Going to Kelmarsh was, I may add, of particular interest, since about ten years before I had been entertained by Nancy Lancaster on two occasions in the wonderful Gallery by Jeffry Wyatville at the back of 39 Brook Street, decorated for her by John Fowler in the late 1950s.[2] I have very fresh memories, first, of a quiet, civilized lunch, and second, a splendidly crowded party.

The Paint Samples

When I visited Kelmarsh, I could only examine those parts of the walls that I could reach from floor level, but I took a total of fifteen paint samples as a 'pilot' exercise in order to explore the evident problem of flaking and obtain a pointer to the decorative history of the room. In particular I hoped to shed light on the relationship between the present John Fowler scheme of about 1950, and that applied by Nancy Lancaster, when as Mrs Ronald Tree she first occupied the house in the second half of the 1920s.

From a purely technical point of view, the samples showed clearly that the plane of weakness from which the flaking on the walls is taking place lies at the junction of the paint with the plaster substrate. It also seems that the problem may be of some standing, since two of the areas sampled lack all layers before those of the 1920s. There appears too to have been a history of redecoration or touching up between the 1920s and the 1950s, suggesting continuous trouble.

Nancy Tree's Scheme

When she first visited the house, Nancy Tree recorded that she found the walls of the Entrance Hall painted 'a dark, rather sad green', and hung with 'dozens of crossed pikes'. In the middle of the room was:[3]

> … a plush roundabout with a *jardinière* at the center … made of the foot of an elephant that someone … must have shot, and planted with a small palm tree.

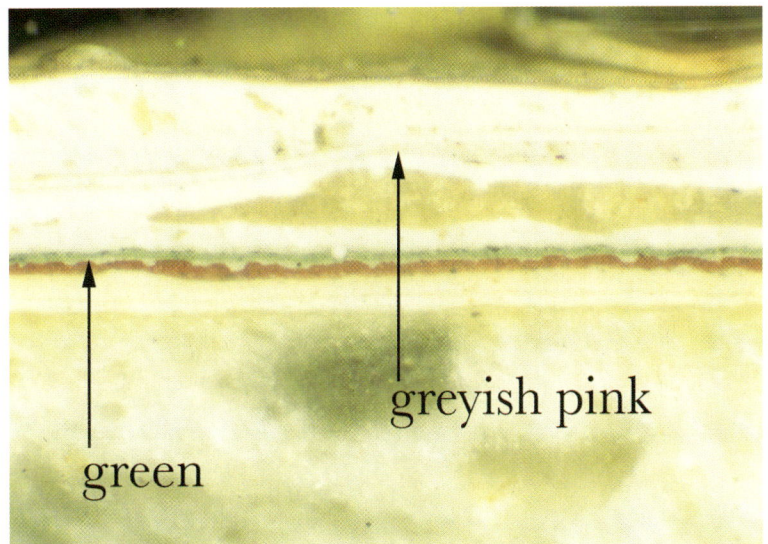

Figure 1 Cross section (×100) of a sample of paint removed from the wall face, Entrance Hall, Kelmarsh.

The effect, she recalled, made her roar with laughter. The green is clearly visible on cross section, and was obliterated by a number of coats of white or pale cream, forming a thick build-up of paint to which a layer of greyish pink was applied.

The latter varies in thickness, but is generally more substantial than the present glaze, and is certainly more delicate in colour. Of course, no assessment of any stipple or other texture can be made from the cross sections, but Mrs Lancaster recorded that the inspiration for the colour was a room at Rushbrooke Hall (near Bury St Edmunds), then occupied by Lady Islington, who '… was the person in England who had the very best taste and the very best color sense'.[4]

The painter she employed in the Entrance Hall at Kelmarsh was introduced to her by her uncle, the architect Paul Phipps, who had been articled to Lutyens before practising both in London and America and who was overseeing the alterations at Kelmarsh. The painter's name was Kick, and she was to work with him on various projects for the next thirty years. He was, she believed:[5]

> … a true genius. He instinctively understood the effect light and shade have on paint in a given room … [and] … could always figure out how to reproduce any color you showed him, and could reproduce it so it had the effect you wanted, which is the point.

Thus, although sent to Rushbrooke to match the pink for use at Kelmarsh, Kick modified it to a tint which she later described as 'an Italian pink, a light terra cotta',[6] but on a sample had looked 'like brown paper'. She also recalled that he applied 'eight coats of distemper in the colour he chose, and the effect was fabulous'.[7] In fact, as the cross sections show, Kick had clearly needed to apply a fair number of coats of white in order to kill the dark green, and had then only applied a comparatively thin coat of pink.

John Fowler's Treatment

The present scheme, executed in about 1950

under John Fowler's direction, comprises one or more coats of white. In conversation with George Ferguson and Marianne Sühr, the painter, Ken Cowens, recalled that Walpamur, an oil-bound distemper, was used, followed by the thin, textured, orange–pink glaze which is still extant.[8]

On most samples there is at least one intermediate scheme between the Tree and Fowler schemes, while some samples have two. Both consist similarly of a white ground and thin glaze, all being more orange in tone than the 1920s scheme, perhaps through matching a discoloured surface. Because of their wide distribution and differing extender content, these layers seem most probably to represent repaints or comprehensive retouchings rather than trials in preparation for the 1950s redecoration, although with only a limited number of samples to hand I have an open mind on this.

Tests on the cross sections show that all layers above the green found by Nancy Tree are lead-free and generally stain strongly for protein. They are thus all likely to have been in Walpamur or a similar oil-bound distemper or 'water paint', an early type of emulsion first introduced in the mid-1870s and widely used for a century until superseded by present-day emulsions (although currently enjoying a revival in some historic-colour ranges).[9] The total thickness of these mid-twentieth-century schemes is, it may be noted, generally equal to, and in some cases substantially greater than, the earlier paint, to which I now turn.

Earlier Schemes

Beneath the green which decorated the walls of the Entrance Hall when Nancy Tree first visited Kelmarsh is a scheme in Pompeian red, which supersedes one in a deep stone colour. On some samples the latter overlies a still earlier scheme in white, but this does not appear consistently, and may have been confined to the western compartment and east face of the arcade. All are in oil and are lead-based.

Before application of the oil schemes, it

appears that most of the plasterwork sampled was unpainted, its smooth eggshell surface indeed suggesting a self-finished material. The notable exception is the plaster of far rougher texture on the outer walls of the western compartment, which was decorated in a succession of size-bound distemper schemes. The earliest layer to survive is in deep yellow, followed by a blue, a green, and a buff, which is succeeded by the oil schemes.

The four samples taken for comparative purposes from the joinery have not been fully examined or correlated with those from the walls. They appear to show a more extensive decorative history than those from the main areas of wall (except, perhaps, those of the western compartment with its distemper layers). This would be consistent with the lower parts of the walls having originally been self-finished. No samples were taken from the ceiling or upper parts of the walls, and for a fuller exploration further sampling is obviously desirable.

Assessment

While the original Gibbs treatment is obviously of very considerable academic interest, in the present context the twentieth-century schemes may have stronger claims in the determination of the future presentation of the Entrance Hall. Evaluation of the importance of the extant Fowler scheme is, however, as yet uncertain: I remain unclear, for instance, as to whether it was formative in his *oeuvre*, or run-of-the-mill; and decisions about the scheme's conservation or reproduction need consideration in the context of the house as a whole. For the moment, therefore, I can only remark on the seemingly greater elegance and restraint of the late 1920s scheme as revealed by the cross sections and the *Country Life* photograph (Ward p. 65, Figure 1). The latter appears to show a single light tone on the ceiling, and far less contrast between the pink on the walls and the various architectural mouldings and ornaments. It accordingly seems likely that the present Fowler scheme represents a

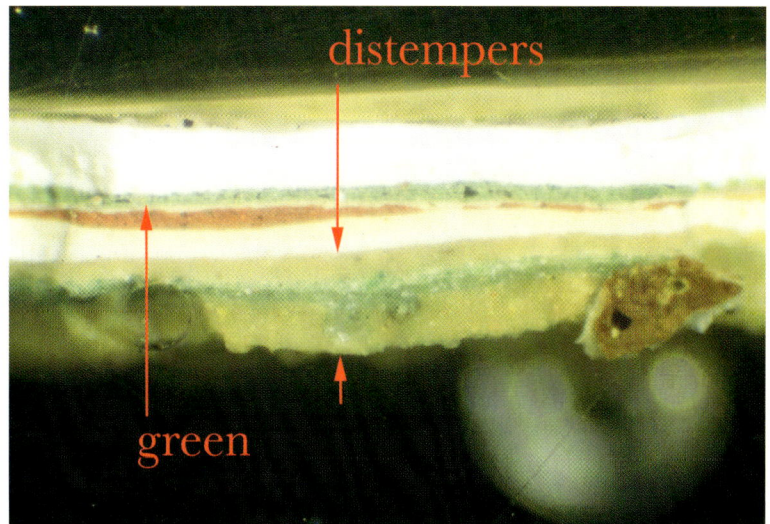

slightly deeper-toned modulation and embellishment of the touched-up, and perhaps slightly discoloured, scheme of the pre-war era.

Although it may not prove easy to establish the precise colour and treatment of the 1920s scheme, it does, I believe, nevertheless have a much stronger claim to importance. Kelmarsh was the house from which Nancy Lancaster's influence initially flowed; it was she who wrought the transformation from the be-piked deep green to a warm welcoming room on whose eagle side-tables by William Kent were placed 'great raffia baskets of clashing pink geraniums'; and it was this decor which Alfred Munnings wanted to paint, with the room filled with hunters returned from the field in red coats.[10] John Fowler and John Cornforth have paid tribute to the vital part the house played before the War in the developing world of country-house decoration and lifestyle,[11] and it was with some pride and amusement that Nancy Lancaster later recorded that '"Kelmarsh Pink" went around the countryside like measles'.[11]

Figure 2 Cross section(x100) of a paint sample removed from the western compartment of the Entrance Hall, Kelmarsh.

References

1 For a brief description, see Friedman, Terry, *James Gibbs*, published for the Paul Mellon Centre for British Studies by Yale University Press, 1984, pp. 125–7, 318.

2 22 Avery Row was the entrance to Nancy Lancaster's private accommodation at the back of the Colefax & Fowler shop on 39 Brook Street.

3 Becker, Robert , *Nancy Lancaster: Her Life, Her World, Her Art*, Alfred A. Knopf, New York, 1996, p. 156.

4 Ibid., p.161. In connection with my paper 'Colour

in Historic Houses in Public Ownership', this volume pp. 41–51, it is worth noting the reliance placed on intuitive taste, as too in Nancy Lancaster's remark 'I supposedly had a very good eye for color' (Becker, *op. cit.*, p. 161)

5 Becker, *op. cit.*, pp. 157–8.

6 Ibid., p. 161.

7 Lancaster, Nancy, unpublished typescript in the archive of Colefax & Fowler, chapter on Kelmarsh.

8 See Sühr, Marianne, 'John Fowler and Nancy Lancaster at Kelmarsh Hall', this volume, pp. 52–8.

9 For a typical formulation, see Heaton, Noel, *Outlines of Paint Technology*, 2nd edition, Charles Griffen, London, 1940, pp. 326–7.

10 Becker, *op. cit.*, pp. 161, 163.

11 Fowler, John and Cornforth, John, *English Decoration in the 18th Century*, Barrie & Jenkins, London, 1974, pp. 17–18; Cornforth, John, *The Inspiration of the Past: Country House Taste in the Twentieth Century*, Viking, London, 1985, pp. 117–119.

12 Lancaster, *op. cit.*

ENGLISH COUNTRY-HOUSE STYLE: THE ENGLISH COUNTRY HOUSE AS IT MIGHT HAVE BEEN BUT NEVER WAS

LOUISE WARD

THIS 'TRADITIONAL' decorating style, so popular in the 1970s and 1980s across the globe, was admired for its (supposed) authenticity and relation to historical country houses. It was in fact a myth – hence the title of this paper – being a manner of decorating which had its origins not centuries, but mere decades before in the ideas and tastes of an American.

This paper focuses on a fiction of English country-house living which came into existence during the inter-war and post-war years; a fictional lifestyle which was the basis of the highly popular English country-house style of decorating in the 1980s. However, in order to understand the development of the English country-house style, it is necessary to acknowledge the wider context from which the country house's identity was drawn.

Throughout its history, the country house has existed as both an architectural entity and a cultural ideal. So much more than a mere building type, it acts as the tangible symbol of a socio-economic and political power structure. Composed of both real and mythic references, the English country house as a cultural ideal communicates both lifestyle and status. In the twentieth century, when country houses were under threat of destruction, the ideal was the subject of much 'fanciful, romanticized … [but] well-articulated veneration'.[1]

The moments of fabrication and reinvention of the English country-house decorating style occur in conjunction with the two key phases of country-house preservation.

In the late nineteenth century decline set in with the agricultural depression, a situation exacerbated by the catastrophic effects of the First World War. However, it was not until the economic and social effects of the inter-war and post-war years and Second World War requisitioning were felt that their loss on a large scale began to be seen as inevitable, and a crisis was forecast for the future of country houses. There was a major shift from this first period of crisis to the second in the mid-1970s, which was caused by the dual effects of taxation and social change. This shift signalled the transformation of the threatened country house from a private, aristocratic home into an integral part, a symbol even, of the national heritage.

Elevated beyond the private home of the privileged, the English country house as a cultural ideal ceased to depend on an attachment to a particular property or even to a particular kind of country house. The idealized symbol was highly problematic, since it included a wide range of periods, building forms, decorating styles, and living patterns. The ideal was epitomized by a house called Brideshead, the fictional creation of Evelyn Waugh in his novel, *Brideshead Revisited*.[2] Brideshead is the ideal of a house which 'grew silently with the centuries, catching and keeping the best of each generation',[3] an ideal expressed inside and outside fiction. Brideshead and its plight epitomized the erosion of a social order and its inherited values – indeed, as Waugh would have it, the impending destruction of civilization. Bound together with an ideal of continuity and family inheritance, the house was not just used as a backdrop, but as a living entity – a palimpsest, with every generation leaving their mark but never totally removing the evidence of what was there before them.

In the 1970s, with the country house under threat of extinction once again, its veneration found new life and reached a far wider audience. It perhaps comes as no surprise that the archetypal Brideshead should have once more played its part, in the form of a television dramatization of the novel.[4] In the context of increasingly non-specific nostalgia for 'the past', this period and the decade that followed witnessed the meteoric rise – indeed the fervent worship – of the country-house ideal. It was an identity constructed from what was seen, what was remembered, and what was imagined or wished to have been. Moving further away from the reality of country-house life and tourism, the country house as an ideal operated as if it had taken on a life of its own, offering evocative glimpses of how life might be lived, or might have been lived.

One example, taken from an American inspirational (or, rather, aspirational) home-decorating book entitled *English Style*, encapsulated the enduring appeal of the English country house:[5]

> There are those for whom the quintessential English interior will always be the grand country house with its enticing clutter, its well-worn upholstery, and its enviable patina of time.

Dressing up rooms in the country-house style was an attempt to capture this evocative myth.

Reassessing the development of the 'heritage' debate shortly after the appearance of his critique *The Heritage Industry*, Robert Hewison offered a useful definition of the nature of a myth:[6]

> … if I describe something as a myth, that does not necessarily mean that it is untrue. Simply, that it is true in a special sense, in that it has truth for a great many people, and this general belief gives it temporary validity. It may contain elements that are unhistorical, or ahistorical, but it adds up to a cultural truth. It

may indeed contain a great deal of historically accurate and factually testable material, but this is transformed into a touchstone of national, local, and even individual, identity.

In the 1980s, the English country house was one such 'touchstone'. While it was being reinvented as a symbol of national heritage, an achievable version of country-house life, a concomitant myth was created in decorating. Effectively, the values encoded in the English country house were transferred to an image of it.

Acting like a veneer which could be applied to the surface of almost any interior, the country-house style of decorating presented a ready-made identity, aspirational and status-laden, to consumers. However, although this style was drawn in part from country houses, such characteristic features as the carefully coordinated riot of ruffles and swags of brightly patterned chintz, the artfully cluttered 'tablescapes', and the pictures hung on ribbons with bows, bear little resemblance to anything seen in English houses before the 1980s.

English country-house style as it existed in the 1980s can be traced back to a very specific source: the American, Nancy Lancaster, a seminal influence on English interior decoration in the mid- to late twentieth century.

Lancaster was born and raised in Virginia, a place which, culturally, socially, and politically, was inextricably tied to its English origins. Indeed, it was said of Lancaster's perspective: 'Anyone quite so authentically English and authentically American could only be a Virginian'.[7]

Lancaster's was a privileged life, with family connections to prominent social networks in both the USA and England.[8] Unquestionably, her upbringing in Virginia, the lifestyle of her family, and her social world were a powerful and lasting source of inspiration which had an enormous effect on her ideas about how one should live. As a result of her education in Europe, time spent in English country houses, and her experience of a decaying colonial civilization in Virginia, Lancaster's notion of 'home' was deeply rooted in grand but domestic houses which had mellowed and showed signs of wear and age.

The notion of domestic comfort espoused by Lancaster went beyond the physical to include the visual and emotional, coalescing in a general sense of 'well-being', a type of 'English comfort' documented by Jane Austen in her novels.

It is interesting to note that Lancaster was not in fact a professional decorator. Although she was deeply involved in the arrangement of her own houses and gave advice to relatives and friends, she did not 'do up' the homes of others. Nevertheless, her series of houses and her ownership of the English decorating firm Colefax & Fowler from the late 1940s place her as the catalyst for the so-called 'English country-house look'.

In decorating, Lancaster was never interested in reproducing period style. It was 'atmosphere' that she sought most of all: patina and the sense of history created by the accretions of family generations. Much of the effect Lancaster was to cultivate with her use of faded fabrics and care-worn objects rests on her non-specific nostalgia for 'romantic disrepair'.[9] Whilst she aspired to create rooms which looked as if they had 'evolved' – as if they had always been there, gradually being improved and mellowed through generations of use – there was a large part of her approach which relied on comforts and conveniences which were not a part of the old English country house.[10]

Lancaster settled permanently in England in the 1920s. Kelmarsh Hall, Northamptonshire, leased between 1926 and 1933, witnessed the introduction of Lancaster's ideas to English houses. It has been said: 'Not only was Kelmarsh well decorated, but it was immensely comfortable, with a bathroom for every bedroom, a novelty in English country houses at that time.'[11] Despite no formal training, Lancaster set new standards and is seen to have been a tremendous influence on those around her – both decorators and house owners. Ditchley in Oxfordshire, where

Figure 1 The Entrance Hall, Kelmarsh Hall, Nancy Lancaster scheme 1928–33. *Country Life Picture Library, 1933*

Lancaster lived from 1933 to 1947, was the house where her talents for decorating really found expression. With the assistance of the French decorator Stéphane Boudin she combined European, English, and American elements to produce interiors which demonstrated to country-house owners (and readers of *Country Life*) an astonishingly new approach. Hers was a manner underpinned by historical knowledge but not in thrall to it. With their bold, bright colours, their blend of informality and elegance, and their combination of period styles – supported by good architectural 'bones' – rooms arranged by Lancaster presented a comfortable, less formal alternative to the historical country house.

The comments of Deborah, Duchess of Devonshire, a woman well versed in English country-house life, offer a fascinating insight into the novelty of the arrangements at Ditchley:[12]

Whatever Nancy touched had that hard-to-pin-down but instantly recognisable gift of

Figure 2 The Hall, Ditchley, water colour 1935. The interiors at Ditchley were painted by Sebriakoff for Country Life. *Country Life Picture Library*

style. Her genius (and that is no exaggeration) was in her eye for colour, scale, objects and the dressing up of them; the stuffs the curtains were made of, their shapes and trimmings … Even the bathrooms were little works of art. Warm, panelled, carpeted … A far cry from the cracked lino and icy draughts to which I was accustomed.

Read in conjunction with contemporary descriptions of draughty English houses, evoked memorably in the journals of James Lees-Milne and in fiction by Evelyn Waugh, it is evident just how inviting and new – in England at least – Lancaster's ideas on comfortable living were. In the light of later imitations it is important to note, however, that such comfort stems not just from the availability of bathrooms and a plethora of soft furnishings but from heat, light, colour, and atmosphere, as well as from all the luxuries a well-run house and supportive staff can offer.

In the 1920s and 1930s, through the influence of modern ideas of space and decorating, there was a general 'clearing up' of the country house with the removal of Edwardian clutter. The Long Gallery at Sudbury Hall, Derbyshire is an interesting example of the life cycle of a historic interior – built as an exercise space and art gallery in the late seventeenth century, it was turned

into a library (Figure 3) then into a cluttered family sitting room and cleared out again in the early twentieth century (Figure 4).[13]

Lancaster offered a manner of decorating and arranging spaces which was not so much a matter of emptying out the grand formal rooms, but making these comfortable as domestic spaces. A contemporary description of her approach can be found in Cecil Beaton's *The Glass of Fashion*, written in 1945:[14]

Among those who energetically flout all contemporary obstacles or disparagements, Mrs Nancy Tree [later Lancaster] has a talent for sprucing up a stately but shabby house and making a grand house less grand. She has an adequate reverence for tradition, observes the rules of style and proportion, and manifests a healthy disregard for the sanctity of 'important' furniture … Her love of colour, her flower sense, and her feeling for comfort have brought a welcome touch to many an English house sorely in need of such ministrations.

At a time when it was in a particularly sorry state, Lancaster offered an alternative to the real English country house, to the consciously arranged 'moderne' interiors of decorators such as Syrie Maugham and the period-style interpretations of those such as Sybil Colefax (1875–1951) and the young John Fowler.

After Lancaster acquired Colefax & Fowler, the firm worked for a very specific clientele under the direction of John Fowler:[15]

> ... clients were all drawn from a small charmed circle; many were Nancy Lancaster's friends and associates, and almost all were untypical of the owners of grand English houses. Many had influential Anglo–American connections and seem to have had access to money that was not typical of the strapped-for-cash owners of great estates and decaying houses of the day.

The look cultivated by Lancaster and followed by patrons of Colefax & Fowler relied on an appreciation of a certain way of living.

The Blue Drawing Room at Chatsworth, by John Fowler of Colefax & Fowler, decorated in the late 1960s is an example of how the firm worked in real country houses for the English aristocracy. There are many elements of this scheme which correspond to the decorating principles of Nancy Lancaster, not least the attention to detail, the quality of the materials, and the feeling of understatement. There are also some of the key devices of the country-house look, such as the ubiquitous skirted table laden with mementos but the look is careworn and relaxed and complements the age and structure of the room.

Here there is an atmosphere which includes, but goes far beyond, the possession of fine antiques and pictures. Lancaster termed this look 'humble elegance' – the shabbiness is just right: not dirty, just pleasantly worn. Fundamentally, there had to be an air of casualness and a disregard for the perceived preciousness of things for it to work.

The interior which best of all demonstrates how Lancaster created her comfortable dream of country-house life is one which is inextricably tied to the myth of 'authenticity' and the paradox of the English country-house style of decorating in following decades. The interior is the Yellow Room.

Ironically, this model, a paragon of its kind to aspirational pursuants of the style, was neither in a house nor in the country. The Yellow Room was the drawing-room-cum-library in Lancaster's *pied-à-terre* above the premises of Colefax & Fowler in London.[16] Originally decorated in 1958–9 by Nancy Lancaster in collaboration with John Fowler, this scheme, with its qualities of understated elegance and faded grandeur, epitomizes the comfortable dream of how life might be lived in an English country house. The Yellow Room was the culmination of Lancaster's

Figure 3 (left) The Long Gallery, Sudbury Hall, Derbyshire, 1905. *Country Life Picture Library*

Figure 4 (right) The Long Gallery, Sudbury Hall, Derbyshire, 1935. *Country Life Picture Library*

Figure 5 The Blue Room,
Chatsworth, late 1960s.
Country Life Picture Library

personal taste and style – it was also the
archetype of the English country-house look
in interior decorating.

The scheme contains many of the elements that were to become clichés of the
popular English country-house style: the
over-scaled curtains, the faux paint effects (in
the marbled cornice and painted husk swags),
the 'tablescapes' consisting of a slender-based
lamp with a pleated shade amid carefully
arranged bibelots, the deeply skirted table
cover, the pictures hung on ribbons and
topped with bows in the eighteenth-century
manner, the mix of grand, formal furniture
with informal and comfortable pieces, and the
density of contents in the room.

The Yellow Room does contain chintz but
not the obviously coordinated wallpaper and
soft furnishings that facilitated the imitative
English country-house style. Colour, scale,
and feeling tie the scheme together, as
opposed to a pedantic adherence to a prede-
termined formula.

The essence of the look has been defined
as: '… a slightly untidy disposition of things
that suggests a life lived spontaneously'.[17]
Although in later years proponents of the
English country-house style were sometimes
overenthusiastic in their cramming of objects
into a room, it could not be said that this
interior was cluttered. Lancaster thought

there should always be things in a room
which were 'warm and ugly' – to give value
to the good things but also to stop 'important' pieces looking too important and a
scheme looking too perfect.[18] Despite the
imposing scale of the room, the chairs are
arranged to suit a few or many people without having to move anything very far; there
is always somewhere to put a drink and
there are lamps to read by – all invisible elements of luxury and comfort. These consid-
erations and, ultimately, the impression that
nothing here is so precious it could not be
touched, or even improved upon by a little
use, make these rooms the epitome of 'humble elegance'.

It is not difficult to understand how this
single interior came to stand for all the
English country-house ideals represented.
There was (and still is) a marked difference
between the care-worn elegance of
Lancaster and the carefully orchestrated
look of Colefax & Fowler. Whilst it could by
no stretch of the imagination be seen as anything other than expensive, mere money
could never have created such a room.

Schemes by John Fowler, such as that created in the early 1960s for the Drawing
Room at Tyninghame demonstrate a frillier
(and much imitated) version of the look
Fowler created with Nancy Lancaster.

Elaborate, highly stylized curtain arrangements are indicative of his style, as is the uses of fabrics where the curtains compensate for a lack of strong architectural detail in the room. While there are similarities to the Yellow Room – not least in the repetition of yellow for walls – these schemes rely on cushions, fabric lampshades, and table covers to create a coherent scheme.

As Lancaster's interiors followed no prescribed (period) formula, they were in fact very difficult to imitate successfully. However, it is not difficult to see how this fantasy could have been taken to be more than an evocation of how life might be lived. The reality is that an American fabricated an identity for the English country-house ideal which was later taken to be both a tradition of aristocratic interior decoration and a

model of Englishness, both in England and abroad.

The potential presented by Lancaster's manner to dress up rooms with a disguise of the past, albeit an imagined past, was exploited extensively in the 1980s, a period perhaps characterized by an overriding obsession with style. It was at this point that the surface identity of the look was lifted away from the underlying principles of proportion, scale, and personal taste which were fundamental to the effect Lancaster aimed for. Lancaster's manner, once converted to a visual style, was popularized through the firm of Colefax & Fowler and through its competitors and imitators. The hallmarks of the English country-house look – as practised by Colefax & Fowler, with whom the look became synonymous – were defined in

Figure 6 The Yellow Room, Avery Row, London, created 1958–9 and photographed for *The World of Interiors* in 1982. *The World of Interiors, September 1982, pp. 94–5, photographer James Mortimer*

Figure 7 Drawing room at 117 E 62nd Street, New York decorated by Mario Buatta in the late 1960s. *By kind permission of Mario Buatta*

1989 by Chester Jones, a decorator with the firm, as:[19]

> Chintz in glorious faded colours, curtains meticulously swagged, fringed and tasselled, the most comfortable upholstery and expertly applied paint finishes, all set in timeless interiors and discreetly lit to show off beautiful antiques and paintings.

Effectively, many of the values encoded within the venerated country-house symbol were transferred to an image of it in the vocabulary of details and objects that constituted the English country-house style.

Through imitation and reinterpretation led by American decorators, such as Mario Buatta and Mark Hampton, a rather different version of the country-house image emerged in the early 1980s – replacing the understated appearance of time-worn elegance with a more polished version.[20] Comparing Mairo Buatta's Fowler-inspired room at 117 E 62nd Street, New York to the Yellow Room it is possible to see how the understated look of Lancaster was admired by American decorators and their clients. However, it was the brighter, more opulent

and fussy look of Fowler which formed the most widely adopted version.

In 1985, Caroline Seebohm highlighted the differences between American and English interpretations of the country-house style and listed the classifying markers:[21]

> With what anticipation does the American visitor set off on his first visit to an English country house, with its history, its architectural authority, its waywardly charming interiors. As he enters the 'drawing room' … with what delight his eye receives the first impressions: light from long, high windows with grand valances ('pelmets'), vases of flowers, chintzes and innumerable paintings, books, memorabilia … But wait. His glance returns to the chintz, so old and worn. To the curtains, taffeta, yes, but faded and unlined. He begins to be distracted by the mixture of styles … More closely examined, a sofa is covered with what must be dog hairs … Books in random piles, unclassified … What can this mean?

Seebohm's imaginary American visitor is taken aback:

> Can this really be the famed original, the prototype from which a decorating legend

sprang? Something seems to have gone wrong – this appears to be some impoverished pastiche rather than the real thing. Let him return to the other side of the Atlantic, to his own, reassuring house, filled with brilliant chintzes, swagged valances, unstinting drapery, eighteenth century-English furniture, its brass fittings polished to a gleam, and lavish accessories – knife cases used for bills and invitations, majolica plates ... Chelsea boxes – all those things that in the United States have come to represent the 'English country-house' look ...

Buatta's oft-photographed yellow Sitting Room – one he acknowledged as his John Fowler copycat scheme – was one of the most influential interiors of the country-house style. Dubbed the 'bows and bow-wows' look, here are all the surface ingredients of the style, with none of the subtlety.

The style had an international appeal and interiors in almost all locations took this controlled, soft furnishings-based, American version as their model. Rooms featured in the glossy pages of magazines and their spin-off books, such as the *House & Garden Book of Classic Rooms* in 1989, are filled with boldly patterned chintz in highly ordered, coordinated schemes – with their use of frills, swags and ruffles, table tops crammed with mementos and pictures hung on ribbons topped with bows. These interiors typify the popular country-house style of the mid- to late 1980s.

As individual components, the elements within the style did not have the potential to signify the ideal, although in the case of chintz it came remarkably close. Most consumers depended on soft furnishings to fill the gaps left by an absence of architectural bones, antique furniture, pictures, and fine decorative objects which fuelled the impression that: 'nothing so symbolizes the English country house interior as chintz'.[22]

This underlines the fact that the English country-house style of the 1980s was not based on an accurate understanding of how English houses were decorated. Relying for its effect upon soft furnishings, this version of the style stands as the antithesis of the

approach developed by Lancaster, but it was the version which was promoted endlessly through photographic representation and magazine coverage. The success of the English country-house style and indeed of interior decorating as a whole in the 1970s and 1980s is intimately connected with the rise of the glossies, magazines which promoted looks and lifestyles and by their nature forced the artificial creation of trends. The pages of magazines such as *House & Garden* and *The World of Interiors* in Britain and *House Beautiful, House & Garden*, and *Architectural Digest* in America provided a catalogue of fantasy environments, images of interiors, and life as it might be.

Imbued with notions of aristocratic tradition, the country-house style had enormous potential for expressing status. Its lack of historical specificity, but powerful aura, served the reinvention and appropriation of identities sought by so many consumers in the 1980s. An insatiable thirst for 'traditional' and 'period' styles reduced the past to a series of visual codes. The theatricality of promissory effect was desired and aspired to, regardless of authenticity or appropriateness. Sampling the entire history of decoration, just as one would rummage through a dressing-up box, decorators and consumers could suggest identities by the use of a few key objects. As we have seen, the repeated use of clichés such as chintz became the language of a style.

Circulating the look to a wider audience of consumers across the globe, the British company Laura Ashley became synonymous with the aspirational, chintzy country-house style. In the home decor text *Laura Ashley Style*, the visual language of the English country house was treated as a defined interior style; however, it was the lifestyle qualities of this enduring decorating tradition which were presented to the consumer:[23]

... the style of decoration associated with the country house is still typified by an eclectic profusion, lovingly assembled over the years.

But it is no longer a set piece of overwhelming grandeur and aesthetic excellence; rather it is

Figure 8 and 9
Laura Ashley style.
*By kind permission of
Laura Ashley Ltd*

a style which exudes an air of comfort and ease, of faded glory and family memorabilia, and above all of quiet good taste.

This passage evokes the country-house style without defining any of its visual characteristics. However, this was not – initially at least – the way in which the style was marketed by Laura Ashley.

Representations of interiors used by Laura Ashley to promote their version of the English country-house style give a clear indication of how an ideal of the aristocratic country house existed alongside popular versions of the style, and how these could be used to serve the same purpose of presenting a total fantasy lifestyle package for consumption. This is also true of their 'how to …' publication, *Laura Ashley Style*, which was intended to trigger desire, suggest possibilities, and give practical advice.

Taking an example from British *House & Garden*, it is possible to see how, in seductive rhetoric, the division was made between the ideal and the enacted style. Whilst magazines placed the style in the public realm and made it available, there is always the sense that the world they represented could never actually be attained. In the introductory essay to *The House & Garden Book of Classic Rooms*, the reason for this was implied:[24]

> A myriad of influences has gone into making these interiors amongst the best of their kind. The major contribution is, of course, the innate taste of so many gifted amateurs and the contributory flair of professional advisers.

Innate taste and flair – these two attributes are as elusive as the country-house ideal. Seen here then is the ability of the country-house ideal (the one actually fabricated by Nancy Lancaster) to carry on existing, almost untouched by the popularity and dissemination of the English country-house style. Similarly, in the book *The World of Interiors*, the editors of the magazine of the same name present the difference between the 'original', which seems to occur as a natural process of living, and the artificiality of the constructed style:[25]

> True clutter is very different from those artfully arranged tablescapes, piles of expensive books and endless buttons and bows aimed to give an instant lived-in look.

Ironically, they published an interior in a New York apartment that is so artfully cluttered and glossy that it is the precise opposite of the shabby elegance of the Yellow Room.

One of the most notable features of this kind of literature is that it did not seem to bother either producers or representers of the style that the country-house life they offered for emulation may not have been at all real. As the country-house look was transformed into a decorating style, it was said that:[26]

> … this is the story of a hoax. Not a whopper, but a misrepresentation, a fantasy of a way of life as seen in its decorating style.

There was little acknowledgement that this

Figure 10 New York apartment decorated in the mid-1980s by Keith Irvine, formerly of Colefax & Fowler. *The World of Interiors, October 1986, pp. 182–3, photographer James Mortimer*

look was not traditional. It was not a 'fantasy of a way of life as seen in its [generic] decorating style', but a fantasy of a way of life seen in a decorating style. One would be led to conclude that, although venerated as a historical, English tradition at all stages of its conception, practice, and reinvention, this fabricated ideal of Englishness was inherently American. Indeed: 'the English country house as it might have been but never was.'[27]

Acknowledgements

This paper is taken from 'Fabricating Tradition', V&A/RCA MA thesis 1996, part of which is published in *Interior Design and Identity*, edited by Penny Sparke, RCA/Manchester University Press, 2004.

References

1 Cannadine, David, *The Pleasures of the Past*, Fontana Press, London, 1990, p. 78.

2 Waugh, Evelyn, *Brideshead Revisited: the Sacred and Profane Memories of Captain Charles Ryder*, Chapman & Hall, London, 1945.

3 Ibid., p. 32.

4 *Brideshead Revisited* was produced by Granada Television in the late 1970s and shown for the first time in 1981. It used, albeit with some artistic licence, Castle Howard in North Yorkshire as the house – which in turn has by this alliance made a great deal of money through tourism. Castle Howard was also used to illustrate the introduction to the catalogue for *The Treasure Houses of Britain* exhibition at the National Gallery of Art, Washington, 1985–6. Once again it is photographed in a heavy mist to evoke an air of supposed decay and endurance through time.

5 Slesin, Susan and Cliff, Stafford, *English Style*, Clarkson Potter Inc., New York, 1984, p. 50.

6 Hewison, Robert, 'Heritage: An Interpretation', in David Uzzell (ed.), *Heritage Interpretation Vol. I*, Belhaven Press, London, 1989. Hewison's earlier text – *The Heritage Industry: Britain in a Climate of Decline* – was published by Methuen in 1987. In a chapter entitled *Brideshead Re-Revisited*, he offered a commentary on the country house as an element of the heritage phenomenon and, interestingly but like so many others, adopted the fictional Brideshead as a model of the English country house.

7 Colefax & Fowler archive, July 1965.

8 For example, one of Lancaster's aunts married into the Astor family, originally from New York but by the late nineteenth century settled in

England. The aunt, Nancy Langhorne, became Lady Astor, the first elected woman member of the House of Commons. Her house, Cliveden, became one of the last great political and social centres of the period.

9 From the Obituary of Nancy Lancaster, *The New York Times*, 22 August 1994.

10 The influx of American heiresses into the English aristocracy in the late nineteenth and early twentieth centuries undoubtedly had implications for the appearance of many houses, as well as a great impact on the installation of amenities such as bathrooms.

11 From the Obituary of Nancy Lancaster in the *Daily Telegraph*, 20 August 1994.

12 Ibid.

13 Sudbury was acquired by the National Trust, and John Fowler of Colefax & Fowler was invited to overhaul the interiors and present them for public opening in the 1960s. Deborah, Duchess of Devonshire, was on the committee that assisted him. The finished rooms were a combination of dramatic, controversial paint use (the white staircase) and subtle, understated restoration where Fowler cleaned but did not alter existing paint schemes.

14 Beaton, Cecil, cited in Cornforth, John, *The Inspiration of the Past: Country House Taste in the Twentieth Century*, Viking, London, 1985, pp. 117–18.

15 Cornforth, John, cited in Calloway, Stephen, *Twentieth Century Decoration*, Weidenfeld & Nicholson, London, 1994, p. 159.

16 22 Avery Row was the entrance to Nancy Lancaster's private accommodation at the back of the Colefax & Fowler shop on 39 Brook Street.

17 Calloway, Stephen and Jones, Stephen, *Traditional Style*, Pyramid Books, London, 1990, p. 170.

18 Richardson, Nancy, 'The Amazing Nancy Lancaster', in *House & Garden* (USA), November 1983, p. 226.

19 Jones, Chester, *Colefax and Fowler, The Best in Interior Decoration*, Barrie & Jenkins, London, 1989, p. 7.

20 In November 1986, *House Beautiful* in America ran a feature called 'Style Makers Today'. Of the seven decorators listed five were working under the aegis of the English country-house style. They were Mario Buatta (very much influenced by John Fowler), Sister Parish (a contemporary of Lancaster), Georgina Fairholme (an English decorator who moved to the States, who had at one time worked with Colefax & Fowler), Mark Hampton (who had worked extensively in England with David Hicks), and David Easton. Testifying to the popularity of the style – if only with magazine editors – a similar outcome was seen in *House & Garden* (USA) in September 1988. Of eight listed, five firms/decorators practised the English country-house style. Within the boundaries of the style their approaches did differ: some were more influenced by the shabbiness of English ideals, whilst others, particularly Buatta, reinvented the style to suit an American audience and thereby created a distinctly foreign look.

21 Seebohm, Caroline, 'To the Manner Born', in *Connoisseur*, vol. ccxiii July 1985, pp. 77–8.

22 Seebohm, Caroline and Sykes, Christopher Simon, *English Country: Living in England's Private Houses*, Clarkson Potter Inc., New York, 1987, p. 117.

23 Gale, Iain and Irvine, Susan, *Laura Ashley Style*, Harmony Books, New York, 1987, p. 50.

24 Harling, Robert, 'Introduction' in: Harling, Robert, Highton, Leone and Bridges, John, *The House and Garden Book of Classic Rooms*, Chatto & Windus, London, 1989, p. 6.

25 Hogg, Minn and Harrop, Wendy, *The World of Interiors*, Conran Octopus, London, 1988.

26 Seebohm, *op. cit.* 1985, p. 78.

27 Taken from an article in the Colefax & Fowler archive, details unknown, dated 1965.

Index